THE TRUTH BEHIND

RACISM
PREJUDICE – A LIFE REVIEW

SIR
ROBERT D. JONES Jr.

THE
TRUTH
BEHIND

PREJUDICE – A LIFE REVIEW

THE TRUTH BEHIND RACISM
Prejudice — A Life Review

Copyright ©

All rights reserved. No part of this book may be reproduced or transmitted in any form or by any means, electronic or mechanical, including photocopying, recording, or by any information storage and retrieval system, without the written permission of the publisher.

Ramtha excerpts: Copyright © 1997, 2000, 2003 JZK, Inc.

The excerpts from Ramtha in this publication are based on Ramtha Dialogues®, a series of magnetic tape recordings registered with the United States Copyright Office, with permission from JZ Knight and JZK, Inc. Ramtha Dialogues® and Ramtha® are trademarks registered with the United States Patent and Trademark Office.

The excerpts from Ramtha are based on the partial transcription of Ramtha Dialogues®, Tape 348, *On Earth As It Is In Heaven*, January 24-26, 1997. Copyright ℗ 1997 JZK, Inc.; Ramtha Dialogues®, Tape 355, *The Plane of Bliss II*, August 8-10, 1997. Copyright ℗ 1997 JZK, Inc.; Tape 469, *Attitudes Vs. The Observer*, September 3, 2000. Copyright ℗ 2000 JZK, Inc.; Tape 480, *The Echo of Discontent – The Enemy Within*, November 24, 2000. Copyright ℗ 2000 JZK, Inc.

C&E[SM], Consciousness & Energy[SM], Fieldwork[SM], The Tank[SM], Blue Body[SM], and Twilight[TM SM] are servicemarks of JZ Knight, d/b/a JZK, Inc., a Washington corporation, and are used with permission.

To my heroes: my mother, Albert Einstein, and JZ Knight.

innocent of prejudice

"So who in this audience is totally innocent of prejudice — prejudice — prejudice against color of skin, color of eyes, cultural dress, color of clothes, color of living standards, prejudice against religion, personal belief? How many people are still Aryans that have a beef against Jews and how many Jews are still living their Jewish days against the Aryans? Prejudice — that women don't know enough, that men know everything, that men think they know everything and we should know something, prejudice against fat people, black people, brown people, red people, green people, white people, women, men, fat, skinny, small, poor, rich, Catholic, Muslim, Jewish, House of Windsor, Republican, Democrat, third party — who in this audience isn't prejudiced?"

— Ramtha

Acknowledgments

I dedicate this book to the heroes in my life.

I dedicate this book to Ramtha, the Master Teacher of the School of Ancient Wisdom. Ramtha has taught me all that I know today about quantum physics, human anatomy, and personal responsibility. Ramtha has taught me that I am responsible for my reality and that God is so loving and unprejudiced that all thoughts manifest. Ramtha has taught me to take my power back and that the journey of this lifetime is to own what was not owned in the last lifetime. Ramtha has taught me that truth is the great equalizer, and Ramtha's greatest teaching is Behold God/man realized and God/woman realized.

I dedicate this book to JZ Knight, who is the great channel of Ramtha, who gives up her life to allow the student body to realize that we are God and that we should not buy into religious hypocrisies, outdated traditions, or the limitations of victimization or woe-is-me.

I dedicate this book to my mother, Zonetta Thompson, who always taught me that I am equal to all people and to not let anyone ever tell me anything different. She taught me that those who judge me know me not and words cannot hurt me.

I also dedicate it to my children, who have come back in this lifetime to be able to teach me because they are wiser than me in this lifetime. Although I may think I am older, like most people think with children, and that I am wiser, the truth of the matter is that my children know better, for they have lived before and already have come back to a new life to make it better. So I dedicate this book to their wisdom as well: my sons Robert IV, Exa-Siltana, my daughters Cozette, Kristynna, and Maisha.

I dedicate this book to Martin Luther King, who was trained and taught how to control people with love. When the people who allowed him to do that realized that it worked, they eliminated him because he had been to the mountaintop and knew the truth. He knew that it was not a mountaintop of God but of control. He knew he would be assassinated. And I honor him, for he knew not the purpose of what he was doing.

And I dedicate this book to Robert F. Kennedy, who many did not know of his generosity to all people, that he did in secret. What greater thing is there than to give or die so another may live more fully?

Sir Robert D. Jones, Jr.

Contents

INTRODUCTION
Beyond the Surface of the Skin — 13

CHAPTER ONE
Creating My Own Prejudice — 21

CHAPTER TWO
*I Have Taken Responsibility
For My Own Creation in This Lifetime
As a Black Man* — 45

CHAPTER THREE
*When You See Everyone As Equal,
You Become Free* — 67

CHAPTER FOUR
*How Blacks Perpetuate Prejudice
Upon Themselves: Light-Skinned
and Dark-Skinned Blacks* — 85

CHAPTER FIVE
A True Story about Prejudice — 103

CHAPTER SIX
Stop Being Black and Be an Individual — 119

LETTERS OF RECOGNITION — 141

SELECTED BIBLIOGRAPHY — 151

INDEX — 153

INTRODUCTION
Beyond the Surface of the Skin

what covers up self is unfinished business

"Now to define ourselves. But also what we learned last night then that self is, in the body of an incarnation like yours, that self when it was on the Plane of Bliss last time — and every time from every incarnation that it arrives there at heaven — is that the great agenda there, the great Judgment Day, the hour of judgment, is to see for ourselves both subjective and objective those aspects of how we placed energy and how ultimately we affected this central core of our being: past-life review, as you like to call it in its flowery, cosmic terms. And what is important about that is that — what we also learned — is that in this hour of judgment there is no one there in heaven, on Bliss, that is the judge. What we are is that ourself. And we have found then that what covers up self is unfinished business."

— Ramtha

I am writing this book because my great Teacher, Ramtha, held a class one day on racism and I could understand what he was saying so clearly that I went up and had a one-on-one with him. I said to him, "Ramtha, I really think that to most people prejudice is a common thing. And a lot of people probably didn't realize they were prejudiced until you brought it out today. And some of them won't face it."

At that point, he said, "You are so correct, Sir Robert. Why do you think you know that so well?"

And I said, "Because I have been prejudiced."

He said, "You are correct." And he said, "Sir Robert, I would like you to write a book from a black man's viewpoint of being prejudiced."

And I said, "So be it."

When he first asked me to do that, I looked at myself and saw how far I have come in twelve years. I no longer had that prejudice I had when I walked into the school twelve years ago. So I thought it was very interesting for him to ask me that.

I wasn't really excited about writing a book until I started thinking about who I was when I first came to the school. I realized that we as a black culture are more prejudiced than white people. We hold onto a two-hundred-year error of prejudice. Then I found plenty of excitement about doing this book because I found that even in my own immediate household, when I wrote the first part of it and said I have a 35,000-year-old Teacher, my wife said, "Robert, if I were you, I would not put that in the book."

And I said, "Why not? It is true."

She said, "But people will think you are crazy."

"Who cares? That is just another prejudice. If it is the truth that my Teacher is 35,000 years old, so be that. I have no problems expressing that because he has never wanted me to worship him or praise him, which was much different than any religion I was exposed to and, believe me, I was exposed to almost all of them. And it is, after all, about speaking the truth. Truth will set you free. So, what, you have a problem with that? After all I am writing this book, not you. They are not going to be looking at you, wondering, doubting, judging, but they will me, and I have noticed a lot of times when we are around certain people and the word Ramtha comes up that you have a lot of doubt, or you move away from the conversation, and many times I have called you on not practicing what he taught us, so I am not surprised for you to have such a comment on something you truly have not yet accepted as true."

Then I called my mother and told her I was going to write a book on prejudice from a black man's perspective. The first thing she said was, "Oh, my God. Why do you have to write that book?" So I knew it was a conflict. When I talked to my next-to-the-oldest sister, she wanted to know why I would write about prejudice: "These white people this, and these white people that." I said she just didn't see it like I see it.

So for my immediate family and my extended family to have so much conflict over the subject matter, I knew I must be onto something. And that is really what motivated me to write the book.

Most people, when they hear the word prejudice, think of racism. But you could be prejudiced against a fat person or a short person or a poor person — any person, place, thing, time, or event. A great deal of this book deals with racism, but prejudice is nothing more than ignorance and fear. What you don't know of somebody or know of a culture, when you have never been around them and don't know how they act or how they eat, how they live, how they think, it is nothing but a sense of fear, born of ignorance. That is all it is.

Some people are afraid of old people. Some people are afraid of children. Others are afraid of sick people. Some of you are prejudiced against meat-eaters or nonmeat-eaters. Some of you have a preference for redheads over blondes. There is Catholic versus Baptist. Even prejudice within our own culture is all the same prejudice, upper-class versus middle-class versus the lower-class people. One thinks they are better than the other; the other cannot understand and is afraid. How can you be so rich and live like that? How can you be so poor and live like that? It is ignorance.

We tend to take things personally — always. When someone treats you badly, the first thing you think is probably that it is because you are black. But if you are white, what is the first thing you think? Maybe that it is because you are a woman. Maybe that person is having a really bad day. Maybe they are just frustrated by your incompetence and not your color. No matter what your color, your gender, your age, we all find a way to think it must be personal. It is about our age or our weight. Maybe it is just the other person's ignorance. Maybe it is just your ignorance. Maybe we just look for reasons to feel bad.

But I think that the majority of blacks always take everything that happens to them from a racial point of view. It is all your choice of perspective, how you want to see things to keep you where you are in your victimization.

Paisley Rekdal, a woman from Seattle who is assistant professor of creative writing at the University of Washington, wrote a book called, *The Night My Mother Met Bruce Lee,* published by Pantheon Books. Rekdal has a Chinese-American mother and a Norwegian father. She talks about growing up with racism in her own family. But one really interesting thing she points out is that she has no way of really knowing why things come at her. She says she has learned not to assume that those slights are racially motivated. She found that when you are prejudiced from the inside from your own family or culture, you can't tell whether it might really be about the differences between generations or genders.

We have learned how to be like this. We have learned to be afraid of what we don't know. Back in 1968, a third-grade teacher in Iowa, a white woman named Jane Elliott, was so moved by the assassination of Martin Luther King, Jr., that she wanted to teach her class about racism. In her own mind, she wanted to know if we are born racist or if we just accept what we are taught. So she told her class of white children that scientists had just discovered that people with blue eyes were smarter and better than people with brown eyes. She suggested that the blue-eyed children shouldn't play with their brown-eyed friends anymore. And she found that fights broke out within minutes. In only a couple of days, she had to tell her class the truth because she could no longer stand to watch how they were treating each other. Our self-image wants to quickly believe and accept anything that will make us feel better about ourselves and better than the people around us. We are very ready to learn prejudice.

I also think we chose to live this lesson because of who we were in our last lifetime. And I am going to explain why I say this. Chances are you were totally opposite in your last lifetime from who you are today. You may be experiencing right now just what you hated before and did not understand, as the laws of evolution and of making known the unknown suggest. This is when the question inevitably arises: How do we define ourselves; what are we, really, beyond all the façades and games that we play?

My work for the last twelve years has been overcoming all of those small thoughts that defined me and kept my life inside a limited box. That gives me a lot to say on the subject because I have learned and I have made overcoming and owning prejudice my truth and wisdom in life. This is what I have learned.

CHAPTER ONE
Creating My Own Prejudice

"And the painful process of taking back one's power often means tripping up the body, its family roots, and pulling out from under it its own rug of blame and jealousy, the dynamics of family situations, pulling the rug out from under sexuality, pulling the rug out from under prejudice, and saying in an unequal yet singular tone, 'I created this. It never was your fault. I made you think it was your fault because that is the coward in me.' "

— Ramtha

I am going back as far as I can remember of my prejudice that I created. As a child, I had an incident where I fell out of a chicken-house window on the farm where I lived. I fell on the concrete and I had glass in my back. I was taken to an emergency hospital in Kansas City.

My first memory — and I imagine I was around eight years of age at that time — is listening to white doctors in the emergency room talk about how the color of the flesh under my black skin was white. I listened to them say they didn't know that black people had white flesh under their colored skin.

Hearing that from doctors in a hospital startled me, scared me tremendously, because here I was at their mercy to take care of me, and what they were discussing was the color of my flesh and my skin. I knew I couldn't go anywhere or do anything, so I was very frightened whether my life was in danger or not. Thank God they stitched my back up — I appreciate that they did that — and I made it out of that situation okay. But it started my thinking that I was different from other people — I was different from white people — and started my looking at myself as a black boy in Kansas City, Kansas.

During this time we were not allowed to be caught out of the house after dark. The danger of a black boy being outside of his house at night where whites lived was that if I were caught alone I could be accused of doing something even if I hadn't done anything. The racism in Kansas City against blacks was phenomenal.

We were always told what the white man would do to black people, how they would punish them, make them do things they didn't want to do. I heard about, had read to me, and saw on television, about what whites would do to blacks if they caught them out at night. They would hang them or they would tar and feather them, which means taking hot tar used for roofing and painting the body all over with it, then putting white feathers on top of that and quite possibly hanging them afterwards. Or they would beat them or drag them behind cars or trucks, or shoot and kill them. I saw pictures of black people being hanged and burned. I remember seeing pictures of the Ku Klux Klan — with the white hoods, the burning crosses — burning families' homes. I remember that the families could never get the police to do anything about it. If the Klan burned a cross in your yard, that meant that you were doomed; and this was as common as the milkman coming around every day. So at a very young age, I knew better than to stay outside after dark.

I heard that there was noplace to eat in the same restaurants, use the same bathrooms, or drink out of the same water faucet as whites. We were not allowed to ride the same bus or live in the same neighborhood or go to the same schools as white people.

So because of these stories and the fear that my mother and my stepfathers had of white people, as a young child I was embedded with a certain amount of fear of whites.

I remember in Kansas City going to Hawthorne School, an all-white school. We moved out of a leaning house with a dirt front yard in the ghetto into a little white neighborhood, a two-story house on a hill, my mother's dream house. I moved there with my mother and my brother and sisters, my stepbrother, my stepsister, and Mr. Matton, my stepfather, to 213 Stewart Street in Kansas City, Kansas. It was a beautiful house with a front yard, and a backyard of grass. We had our own driveway and our own garage and a basement.

I remember moving there around 1953 and being the only blacks in the neighborhood. And I remember the night and the day of moving in. The whites would drive by and say to us, "Why don't you niggers go back to where you come from and get out of our neighborhood? We don't want you in our neighborhood. Take your black asses back to where you come from."

I remember my mother saying, "Pay no attention to them." And I remember saying, "How can you not pay attention to them? They are talking to us." My mother said they were just ignorant. People threw rocks up on our porch at night and through the big picture window in our front room. I remember my mother calling the police, and they would never come. All the policemen were white at that time.

I was scared to go to the neighborhood grocery store, which was owned by whites, because they always wanted to know what we black kids were doing in that neighborhood. Sometimes they would allow us to buy in those stores and sometimes they wouldn't. Going to the store was one of our biggest challenges because walking in the neighborhood, we would get beat up or get our money taken from us. Coming back from the store, they would take our groceries from us.

We would come home beat up, crying to our parents, and it always made my stepfather angry. He would always tell us that if we came home and let somebody beat us up and take our money or take our food, that he was going to "whop our asses." And he did a lot of times, because white kids and white adults would come out of their houses and run us down the street, sic their dogs on us, snatch the bags, break the milk, or open the packages and throw them on the ground. After this happened two or three times, we always had to go to the store with one of the brothers or sisters. We could never go to the store alone. That angered me tremendously.

Then I remember going to Hawthorne Elementary School, being the very first black family to go to that school. The teachers always made me sit in the back of the room or sit on the dunce stools because I was considered stupid. I remember that I felt the white teachers never gave me a chance to be able to do anything like everybody else.

During playtime we could only play amongst ourselves because the white kids would not play with us, would not eat in the lunchroom beside us. We had our own separate table. They would always pick fights with us, and we came from a home where we did not fight, but we learned how to fight real quick. And my stepfather taught us how to fight, how to stand up for ourselves, and how to protect one another.

I remember that even what we ate at lunch was so mystical to the students around us and even to the teachers. I remember them just feeling my woolly hair and saying that it is soft. I remember that touching them, brushing up against them or falling against them in any kind of way, the reaction was like I was poison, like, "Nigger don't touch me; get away from me." That puzzled me. And it made me, even as a child, say where is God? Why would God let this happen?

I remember coming home from school, all of us having to wait for each other in front of the office. We would join hands together and put the youngest one in the center of the circle and walk home like that because the white adults as well as the white kids would always throw rocks, hit us, spit on us, and kick at us all the way home. It was less than a half-mile from my front door to the school, and every day there would be a bunch of white kids on the corner, waiting for us to come that way. Sometimes we even had to be taken home by the principal or wait for our parents to come and pick us up because the brutalization was so constant.

I remember that I was in special education in the special resources department in the school basement. It was nothing but a holding tank for those considered stupid. We were not allowed to go out at the same time that the rest of the school went for recess. We went after everyone else.

I will never forget when the second black family moved into the neighborhood. They moved in right across the street from us. I was so happy to see more forces come onto the block. And we got to know one another straightaway and

CREATING MY OWN PREJUDICE

we became friends. Shortly thereafter other blacks moved into the neighborhood. It seemed that as soon as we moved into that neighborhood, the whites started moving out. They said that for blacks to live in their neighborhood brought down the property value.

By this time I was starting to have a great prejudice, a great hatred for white people. Their prejudice angered me because they always felt that they were better than we were, and we always spent time trying to prove that they weren't better. Or we were always submissive to the white boy or white girl because of what would happen to us if we even got caught looking them in the eye. I will never forget that in order to talk to our instructors or to talk to white boys, we always had to look down at the ground. We were always taught never to look at a white person in the eyes, and we had to talk to them looking down at the floor and never look up in their eyes. I really hated that. It made me feel degraded as a kid. But I did it because I was taught to do so. But then as I grew older, because I knew it was something I wasn't supposed to do, I took it on every chance I could get to stare at them in the eyes, because I noticed when you looked at people in their eyes — mainly white people — they felt a sense of fear from a black person staring them in the eyes.

But still I watched white people: When they talk to you, they are always in your face and they are staring you in your eyes. I noticed that when white people talked to other people, they would make eye-to-eye contact. So I learned from them that that was a sense of power. And so I started doing that to the degree that, with my teachers — especially in Catholic school, with the nuns — I would stare them in the eyes and a lot of times wouldn't say anything. But they knew from my eyes that it meant bad news or good news, just by my looking at them.

I recently had a white woman explain to me that it is the same thing for women, that when they walk down the street they just don't make contact with a man's eyes because it is considered an invitation, an encouragement in some kind of way to respond to them. In order to feel safe, a woman has to avoid making eye contact, just like we had to do as children.

I never had fear of the white man unless there were two or three of them. But one-on-one, I never had a fear of a white man because I have always been big and I just felt like I could handle myself. But I was scared to death of white women, from watching so many black men being destroyed by looking at white women or talking to white women. And so then you are in a situation where you are damned if you do and damned if you don't, because one of the things that white women were always taught was that black men are generously "endowed." And so then if a white woman wanted to make love to a black man she would say, "If you don't, I will holler rape." Well, if you got caught making love to a white woman back then, you were dead. And if a white woman hollered "rape" or "the black man touched me," you were dead too. If you said no, she could yell anyway. So I made it my job never, ever to be in a situation one-on-one with a white woman — never.

There were even times going to work at the Italian restaurant that I worked in — the men's and women's bathrooms were side by side but there was a hallway — when I passed women in that hallway, I always looked down and looked the opposite way, like I didn't see them, like they didn't exist, because of the fear. I was in my forties before I would even consider dealing with a white woman.

So I grew up hating white people because there were more of them where I lived, because they were better than I was, and because of the abuse.

My mother worked for white people, cooking in their house. I remember taking my mother to work with my sister or my brothers when even just driving in an all-white neighborhood the police would stop us and think we were there to do some wrong. We always had to prove that my mother was merely going to work.

I never liked the fact that my mother had to work for white people, cook for them, clean for them, and always go in the back door. She was never allowed to go in the front door. I remember going with my mother many times, sitting out in the car, sleeping in the car, while she was in the house cooking or cleaning. I remember when she cooked for big parties, she used to bring home delicious meals after the whites were through — leftovers. But I never complained because it was more exquisite than we had ever had before.

I remember cutting grass for the family that my mother worked for, and raking leaves for them, and getting paid a little bit of nothing, maybe a meal for my labor. I was allowed to sit at the back door and my mother would bring me something to eat out there, after she got permission to feed me after I had worked all day. I remember one time going into the house, into the kitchen through the back, and the owner of the house came in and scolded both my mother and me. I was told never to come in again, that outside the back door was my place. That made me very angry.

My mother got another job working for a Jewish family. It was basically the same thing. They had a little bit more tolerance for us. We could come in as far as the kitchen.

I was always curious about why white people didn't have any color and why they had blue eyes or green eyes or black eyes, why they had blond or brown or black hair with pale white skin. Who were they? What were they? Why did they look like this?

And at the same time, I was so confused because I was always taught that Jesus Christ was our savior. But they always portrayed Jesus with blond hair and blue eyes, a white man like the very ones that I was afraid of, the very ones that used to beat me up, used to beat my sisters up, used to take our groceries and our money, used to throw rocks and spit and say that we weren't good enough to be around them, that hated us because we lived in their neighborhood. It confused me as to the whole concept of Christ. Why would Christ be white? Why wouldn't he be black or multicolored or every color? Why was he only white and blue-eyed with light hair? This was the entity that the preacher in the Baptist Church, the Christian Church, and also the Catholic Church said was my savior; but I could never understand that.

At the same time, I could never understand why only certain people were chosen to be ministers, preachers, to be the Pope. How could any of them be better than me? And to me, all of them in the Baptist and the Christian and the Catholic churches all said that they were chosen — meaning that they were better than me because I was not chosen. So I was also prejudiced against different churches and religion as a whole.

My prejudice started off with the Baptist Church. Here there was a minister who said he was chosen by God. I understood that made me less than what he was, but I never accepted that. I watched him play inappropriately with little girls my age and had no respect for him. I did not feel he could be chosen. I remember telling my mother that the minister liked my girlfriend at that time. Naturally, that was blasphemy. Later I found out that he did try to molest her, so I didn't have any respect for those who told us one thing and did another.

I also had no respect for the Catholic Church because the priests and the Pope were so special — which made everybody else less-than — so special that we were made to confess our sins to them. Many times I went in to confess my sins and asked the father whom he told his sins to. When he said, "Child, I confess my sins to God," I said, "Why can't I do the same? What makes you so special to be between me and God?" This created a prejudice in me against the priests.

I also tried the Seventh Day Adventist Church. Again I saw that I was required to follow the agenda of the minister who went against his own agenda, once again saying he was special and he was chosen. How could these ministers be better than me but still be doing the same stuff I was doing, even if I was doing it on a heavier level?

I never felt bad about my prejudice. I thought my questions to the ministers were simple: Have you ever seen God? You say we live eternal life, but have you died and lived eternal life? Have you ever been to hell? The answers were always no. They were preaching what they hadn't experienced, so I had trouble believing. I also had trouble with how important it was to raise a certain amount of money when the ministers lived in big, nice houses and drove big, nice cars.

One of my greatest learnings was in the Baptist Sunday School when I kept telling them I could not read and they kept demanding that I read. I read "God" as "dog" because that is how I saw it. They considered it a damnation. I was sinning and the devil was in me. But this is what I saw with my eyes. This certainly added to my anger and my prejudice.

Growing up in a family of eleven sisters and brothers, all of them being A and B students, I was the only one that would have challenges just being able to read or write the alphabet. I remember in the kindergarten class that I was always made fun of because I did not talk until the age of seven. Some people call it tongue-tie, or lift tongue. Either way, when I spoke, it was incoherent. A lot of times when I spoke I would say things like, "me wanted to go to the bathroom," or "me was hungry," or "me need help." That's when I could get words out.

So going through school from the kindergarten — which I failed twice — to the eighth grade, I was always getting in trouble, never being able to read, write, or spell, or do math, never being able to accomplish the tasks in written form, but if I was asked a question out loud, I always answered correctly. They were always puzzled; if I could not read it, where did I get it? So going as far as the eighth grade — praying every day to God to teach me how to read, write, and spell — I had a daily prayer before I went to bed at night.

Twenty-nine years later, one day I was sitting on the beach — and I always used to carry a tape recorder around with me — and I remember a lady friend of mine telling me the correct way to spell her name, Michelle. And I traced it in the sand as she was telling me how to spell it. She wrote it in the sand and I traced over it. And lo and behold, three hours later I could remember the first three letters of her name and I could write it. The next day, after I continued tracing it on the sand early one morning, I recalled the whole spelling of the name. So I knew then that touching it, seeing it, and feeling it had some type of connection.

At the age of twenty-two, I was just coming out of Vietnam. I went to Vietnam. And I clearly remember going to the recruiting station telling them that I wanted to join the service, and they told me I had to take a test. I told them I could not read or spell and they asked me how bad did I want to go. At that time I was facing a choice to go to the service or go to jail. I had created a little petty theft. You know how it is. So therefore, I told them I wanted to go very badly. It was very important that I go. I had never been to jail and didn't want to experience it then. So they told me to have a seat. About twenty-five minutes later the sergeant came back with the test — sergeant or lieutenant; I can't remember which — told me to sign on the dotted line. And he said "By the way, if you can't spell your name, just put an 'X.'" So I signed my name, the one thing I could do. It was brilliant to go to the army to get an education, I thought.

So I went through basic training, which was disgusting, and I went to combat training. And so then I thought that my career would be to go to college, or go to school and learn how to learn. But, Lord, what I found out was that they had big plans for me to go straight to Vietnam because I was a mean fighting machine. I said, "Oh, my God, my God, what have I gotten myself into?" But I was always the type of soldier that volunteered to be the one that they use on any training, to teach the others how to properly execute, so I knew it well, I knew, and I just knew. And I told my mother, "Don't worry about me; I will come back as a whole human, breathing as you see me today." And I did.

So getting out of the service: It took me three and a half years to do two years, and those of you who have ever been in the service know that I must have been a naughty boy. But I made it with an honorable discharge up under honorable conditions. And the first thing, using the GI Bill for education, I went to an adult high school and enrolled and within three months they told me they could no longer take the government money because, for whatever reason, I would learn something one day and the next it was like I had never seen it before. The Veterans Administration then did a series of tests on me. It was four hours a day for five days straight, and they discovered that I had six of the seven known types of dyslexia, meaning there are six different types and the seventh is a combination of all six. They reminded me that Einstein only had one, so I could forget it, and told me that I would never be anything but a janitor and that I would never learn to read or spell.

So then, once again, with my tape recorder, I found myself going to the woods and the mountains asking God to show me a way. Once again it came back that if I could "see it, say it, hear it, and feel it" simultaneously, that would allow me to be able to read and spell anything. And so I created this method by using white index cards with black crayon, writing the word boldly and putting on top of the index card "see it, say it, hear it, feel it." When I say feel it, I mean feel it with your finger. Therefore I was using all my senses simultaneously and creating new neuronets in the brain. And I would do this three times on the front side of the card, and then I would turn the card over, and at the top of the card, it would say, "See it, say it, write it" — see it, say it, write it. And also you were hearing it at the same time, and I would do this elongating the word, not breaking the word down into syllables but feeling over the word as I would say the word simultaneously. One of the hardest things for people with learning problems, mainly dyslexia, is to see and hear the individual letters of the words.

Right about this time, my benefits had run out. So then, I went to Social Security rehabilitation and convinced them that I had a program that could teach me how to read, write, and spell. And they paid for me to hire a teacher that would take me through this program that I created, and told me that they would only pay for it if I could show results every five days. And for two years, one to two hours a day, the instructor took me through this program. It was new for her and new for me as well. But we showed them that at the beginning of the week she would give me words that I could not read or spell, and at the end of five days of using this process, these words were within my long-term memory for life. Any one of these words that did not stick were added to the list the following week. We started off with ten words and ended up with as many as fifty words a week. And I went from not being able to read the alphabet or write to an eighth- or ninth-grade level of reading, writing, and spelling.

Then rehab told me they no longer would pay because most things are written on a seventh-grade level and I achieved beyond that. So that was the end of that party. So I continued to do the program by myself and took myself to a college level.

I also started working with kids and adults with the seven different types of dyslexia, and using the same method, I produced the same results I achieved for myself. To this day, I have the I Beat Dyslexia Center in Yelm, Washington, where I work with children one on one with great joy. Check our Web site at www.ibeatdyslexia.com. I have had endorsements across the board from former President Bill Clinton, to senators and Congresspersons, teachers, educators, parents, and children who are now successful and happy in their professions. I have been doing this since 1979, and I have written a book about my life story on dyslexia. In this book I describe the method day by day, from the beginning to the end, with other techniques in it as well. The name of the book is *I Beat Dyslexia, So Can You*, by JZK

Publishing. The Church did not teach me how to read the word God correctly and stop seeing it as dog in my brain. I figured a way out myself and it worked.

I remember that our church, Calvary Baptist Church, was all blacks, no whites. So not only did we have our black schools, our black neighborhoods, we had black churches. But we did not have our black banks, our black leaders. We did not have black teachers or politicians or policemen. This wasn't the 1800s. This was the forties and fifties in America, the land of the free. But I grew to see it as the land of a conservative communism that controls everybody and everything. And the majority — which is considered the minority, people of color — are underdogs. Yes, I was prejudiced. Yes, I hated any race but the black race, because on every level I was brought up on as a kid I was taught nothing but fear for the white man.

I could never understand in the Catholic Church, when they would do the ceremony in Latin and ask you to agree to it, I always felt that they could be saying anything and why should I agree? I couldn't speak Latin or read Latin, so I had a real challenge and a great deal of prejudice about them imposing something on a group of people who they knew had no knowledge of what they were saying.

And all of the nuns and priests were white; black nuns and priests were unheard of then. In the Catholic schools they would rap your knuckles, twist your hair, pull your hair, or put you in a corner if you could not perform at the level of everyone else. I was certainly prejudiced against them. I saw no balance in them at all, dressed in black, so crisp and clean, so righteous and yet, as far as I could see, so full of falseness. Yet it was obvious that the men had power over the women, that the women were not equal to the men. There were no women priests, only nuns. I was wise enough to see that because I was raised mostly by women. They were great, powerful, consistent beings, and I resented it that the Catholic Church's men thought they were better than women.

They never talked about the daughter of God. If God is in all of us, why have religions never expressed the equality of all of us becoming God? They taught that you would be condemned to hell if you didn't do as the priests taught; I resented that idea. And you find more women in churches than men. Women are looking for someone, something to depend upon, and the church knows they are gullible.

Churches don't teach the true path to God because they know that men and women will realize that God truly exists within themselves. People would have no use for a minister, a pope, a preacher. The church knows that God fully realized within women as well as men would not continue to give their money to a church, chosen to be "special" to perform the deeds of God — making everyone else less-than. If the church tells you this, it ends the money. They have to teach heaven — good — and hell — bad — in order to control you. Ask them if they will be judged for their own sins. They will tell you they have no sins, that they were chosen by God.

I saw these things. I saw the church play the same games on us that they told us not to play on other people. And I did not have a man in my life to take care of me. I looked up to only women in my young life.

I was taught as a kid that when you speak to the whites, you must say yes, sir; no, sir; yes, ma'am. When we said this to our own culture, to me it was only a respect thing, that our elders made us respect them by saying sir and ma'am, and I saw nothing wrong with that. But when it came to the white race, it felt like a different agenda. It was forced respect, and I resented it.

The more blacks that moved into the neighborhood, the bigger the warfare became and the more the whites hated the blacks coming into their neighborhood. The blacks then became more in numbers and more powerful, and there were fights every day between the blacks and the whites. The difference in the two sides was that the whites would be white adults as well as kids; there were no black adults, so we were outnumbered. Yes, I hated it.

I was angry watching my mother so afraid of white people, watching my brothers and sisters being so afraid of them. Even when she was right, my mother was afraid to say she was right to a white man, or if she was trying to get something, she might not get it if she spoke up.

I remember what they called the white trash: the white people who did not feel they were better or less than the black people. They did not have what the middle-class and upper-class whites had. They were also considered white trash because they played with and communicated with blacks. But most of those were truly friends and truly saw no difference in colors or conditions of living because they were right there with us, living, eating, and surviving the same way we were.

But I was taught that the middle and upper class were superior. They became the presidents; they ruled the world. They were the police, the government, the school system. They were the judges and the attorneys. We had to always recognize where we came from and that these white people were superior, that we must always do as they said if we wanted to get anywhere in the world. If we wanted to be even a third of what they were, we were to be submissive to them.

Oh, yes, I hated them. I thought they were crazy. I was saying what kind of a world is this? Why would God make such a world? This was why I couldn't humble myself to say Christ was my savior. Even black churches had a white man with blue eyes on the cross. There was no brown man with brown, woolly hair. Was the savior of my everyday life a white man with blue eyes that would cuss you, beat you, burn you, kill you? Most black people in my era were confused by this. It made no sense.

You know, when you see a blonde-haired beauty with blue or green eyes, you can't help but look at them twice. Who are they? Where do they come from? Am I the minority or am I the majority? I always felt that they were superior because the symbol on the cross was blond-haired with greenish-blue eyes and a white body. So it made me really think that maybe I was out of place, because if God's only begotten son was white, maybe we did have to have permission to live in certain place, ride certain buses, or to eat at the same restaurant with the blue eyes and blond hair. This was the message given to me as a child.

All the books were written with characters of white skin, not brown — no Japanese, Chinese, Filipino, Korean — just white. Even the storybooks were all white.

I ask the white man or woman, "How would you have dealt with this? Would you have been confused? Would you have been prejudiced? Would you have felt you had equal rights?" I don't think so. I am a six-foot-three black man with dreadlocks, telling my story about a life of prejudice. I, as a black man, was more prejudiced than any white person could ever be. I was taught that whatever whites say is right. Imagine that issue in this lifetime.

Going to high school in the fifties, we had more light-skinned black teachers. They had degrees, they could teach, and they were prejudiced against white people because they were not making the salary that the white man was making. They were also prejudiced against darker black people because they felt that the dark-skinned people, their blackness, was the reason for their failure. I even had a prejudice against light-skinned black people. And I am not considered black-skinned, I am what is considered brown-skinned. I had some black-skinned relatives, but that made no difference.

Much of my prejudice was because I was ignorant and so confused about who was who. But as life went on and I saw all these scenarios happening around me, I had to, as a black man, find out who I was and my place in life. Why was I here? What was my journey?

I remember clearly resenting all of the white teachers because they couldn't teach me. They didn't know what was wrong with me. They didn't know why I couldn't read, why I couldn't spell. And I held a grudge against them, thinking that they didn't teach me because they didn't want to teach me and they wanted me to be ignorant, that they didn't want me to learn. I found out later that was not the case at all.

But I had created something in this lifetime that the majority of the people in this lifetime, because of their color, don't know how to deal with today. I didn't know it then; I was a victim. It is easier to be a victim than to stand your ground. It is easier to be less than, than to stand your ground and be equal.

I remember later going to war, to Vietnam. I joined to learn to read and spell like everybody else. That was eye-opening. The first unit that I joined up for — being the only black in the infantry unit, being the only black in basic training, being the very first black in phase two of the service, when your profession is decided — was my first experience having a white friend. He was from Louisiana. I don't know why or how we became such close friends, but if any white boy would say anything about me, he would kick their ass — and he could, so well that most white boys were afraid of him. This was the first white boy that I recognized as a friend, and we met in basic training. I don't know why he did what he did. I don't know why we were so close, but his defense of me was the moment that I realized that not all whites were prejudiced against blacks.

We were assigned to the same infantry unit in Vietnam and even there, when the whites outnumbered the blacks, this white friend stayed a friend and stayed by my side. We treated each other as equals. We used to walk point together, and I could trust that he would go hard and protect my back. We ate out of the same can of C rations. We shared with one another. When I didn't have water, he gave me some of his water. He was the first true friend I ever had.

I was still prejudiced toward other white people. I didn't trust them and I was afraid of them. I slept with my pistol every night and I really hated them. But I felt that this white boy had a black soul. Now soul doesn't have a color, and this shouldn't be interpreted as a prejudice statement. But he was the very first white person that ever called me brother. We used to talk about how he didn't like being white. He said he felt like a black man in a white body. This boy was a bridge for me because there was no difference from me in the way he acted, what he liked to eat, the way he talked. He was from the South, so I imagine now that it was a Southern, cultural thing. No whites that I knew of in Kansas City ate soul food and corn bread. Anyway, we loved and respected one another; we looked after one another.

One of his greatest dreams was to be able to finish his tour and go back down South and buy a motorcycle, a Harley Davidson. But one day we were walking point and he walked over a booby trap and it blew off his legs. It didn't kill him but it took his dream from him. The last time I ever saw him was when he was medivacked out, but I love him to this day. I hope he is still the warrior that he was. If you read this story, please contact me.

There was a great deal of prejudice in the war. The black men were almost like war machines that would fight. Ninety percent of the white men wanted to be in a unit with black men because we were notorious fighters with no fear. We didn't give a damn. We smoked marijuana and we did whatever it took, but we got the job done. And all the white boys knew that nine out of ten, the blacks would be leading and they would get you through.

The sergeants, captains, second lieutenants were all white, but it made no difference to the black man. He had a job to do and he did that job. I certainly was prejudiced against white superiors because they almost always put us out there in the front, and they were always behind. To us, they had no courage. There were a few out front fighting. But we did our job well, and a lot of us died.

I never will forget in basic training, if you came from Kansas City, New York City, Philadelphia, or Chicago and you were black, you were without a doubt in the front line. You will find this in history. They took us from the prisons and jails and sent us to Vietnam because we were fighting machines. And in Vietnam the white boys started seeing us as equal to them, and in many instances saw that we were better than them.

Vietnam was the greatest time in my life because most of the time I didn't do what they told me to do. I did what I wanted to do. For once I felt on equal ground to the white man: They had .45s, I had a .45; they had M-16s, I had the M-16; they had grenades, I had grenades; and I had their respect as an equal.

During the sixties I was very militant. In Vietnam I had a chance to see how truly prejudiced the white man was, and not only against blacks. I ignorantly thought that he was prejudiced only against the black man, but I got to see the same prejudice and the same superiority over the Vietnamese, and I hated to see their abuse. So I gladly fought a war against the Vietcong and I fought a war against the white boy, against prejudice, because we had been so misled.

Ignorance, a lack of knowledge, is humanity's greatest downfall: It makes us passive enough to believe, keeps us from taking responsibility for who and what we are, and lets us be led into hating another culture or another color. It leaves a handful to rule the world. Thank God I have learned freedom and the power of wisdom and knowledge from my Teacher, Ramtha. The more you desire to have knowledge, the freer you will become: You will be able to see farther than your eyes, hear farther than your ears.

How did we determine a Vietcong from a Vietnamese? By those who wore regular clothes. Those who wore pajamas at night were considered Vietcong, a traitor. And what I realized was that I never felt righteous in that war. When you have young children come up to you and say, "Di vê" — "go home" in Vietnamese — what they are saying is, "Black man, go home. It is not your war. We are brothers." And we heard that from so many people. It really made me wonder why I was there, why I was killing those innocent people. I realized later that the whole political war was a fight between two brothers; Americans and Vietnamese died over a family feud.

I would be willing to experience my prejudice and my ignorance all over again, because everything, every moment of my life, I created for a great learning experience. I could accept someone to think they are greater than me just to come to the point I have arrived at this day: to know that God is all colors, all races, and that God lies in the depths of all of our souls. God is equal to all. If this is what it takes in this lifetime for me to come to this realization, I would do it all again. I never have any regrets. I have most definitely learned.

CHAPTER TWO
I Have Taken Responsibility
For My Own Creation in This Lifetime
As a Black Man

your greatest victory

"So who are you going to be when you die? You go back to the light. All of this is going to be in your light review. I swear upon my soul, 'tis so. And what are you going to see? Only an effort. This life was nothing more than an effort to become greater. This life was to understand prejudice. This life was to be prejudice. This life was to understand. This life was not only to become what you despised previously but to be it in a way that you could understand it. And your greatest victory was to live this life to its greatest nobility, not its greatest shame."

— Ramtha

I have contemplated and understood, from over a decade of studying the teachings with a great Teacher named Ramtha the Enlightened One and from the beautiful lady JZ Knight who channels Ramtha, that I chose who I am in this lifetime. Before I incarnated into this life, when I was on the Plane of Bliss, I chose all of the players in this lifetime.

In 1988, a friend of mine shared with me some videos and cassette tapes about JZ Knight and Ramtha. I spent about twelve hours looking at six videos, and listening to cassette tapes. They had one particular video with JZ Knight and Ramtha in Hawaii, and you actually see Ramtha taking over her body. That was the most amazing thing I have seen in my life, and watching those videos and listening to the cassette tapes, I knew that I wanted to go see Ramtha — I called him he, she, or whatever — and so three months later Ramtha's School of Enlightenment had scheduled a Beginning Consciousness & Energy℠ Workshop weekend in Yelm, Washington, and I showed up.

When I was first introduced to these videos, and after I had seen them, I told my friend that I would say something to him, and he would have to swear he would never tell anyone, and he swore. I had known him for about fifteen years, and I knew he would keep his word. So what I told him was, "I want to go see this JZ/Ramtha person, and when I see him, I want him to look me in the eyes and touch me."

As I said before, three months later I was at the School of Ancient Wisdom's Retreat. There were about fifteen hundred people there from all over the world. And he walked up to me amongst all fifteen hundred people, came straight to me, looked me in the eyes, and kissed the front and back of my hand, and each side of my face and my forehead, and I thought I was going to have an accident in my pants.

After that event, I called my friend in Baltimore and told him what had happened, and he swore he had never said anything to anyone. For the next three months, every time I was in the audience, which was every event, the Ram did the same thing. And I knew the only person who could be in Baltimore and Yelm at the same time had to be God. So I had no doubt: When he looks in your eyes, he penetrates every cell in your body, and you know that this is not a woman, and you know this is not a man on this earth.

So in the first C&E^{SM} Workshop weekend, one of the things we were taught was how to manifest three things we wanted. There was only one thing I wanted at that time, to be a part of the staff and be in that school whenever this God-entity came to this earth. And so I did what he told me to do just like he told everyone else: that consciousness and energy create the nature of reality; Behold God — that we are God/man and God/woman endeavoring to become realized — that we are the creator and the manifester of our reality; that all we create we are responsible for manifesting in our life, and as we create it, if we don't like it, we can uncreate it, because we are forgotten Gods that are back on this plane for an unfinished business that we did not complete in our other lifetimes. Blame no people, places, things, times or events, as Ramtha has taught, for anything that happens to us in our life, but take full responsibility, for we created it as a learning experience.

And within three months, after sending my résumé and writing a letter to JZ, I was called in for an interview for the position of guarding JZ while channeling Ramtha. So I became a Red Guard, as it is called, that guards and protects JZ's body and the students in the school. Ramtha needs no one to guard him. Once again the consciousness and energy of my desire during that Beginning Workshop was fulfilled. I have been there for fourteen-and-a-half years, maybe missing only three weeks of classes, and I am stretching it at that.

One of my greatest teachings from Ramtha is the truth teachings. Speaking truth and living truth really will set you free. Care not what anyone thinks of you is what I learned. Accept the truth, face the truth, change it if you desire, and you will be changed for the rest of your life.

Ramtha, I see him like my father that I never had in this lifetime. I was raised by my mother and seven women in the family. JZ Knight is someone that I honor highly and respect to the highest level and love greatly to the best of my ability. She has always spoken the truth to me and always told it as it is, whether I wanted to hear it or not, just like my mother or my sisters would do. The difference between JZ Knight and my mother or sisters is my mother or sisters would sometimes add a curve to the truth, which sometimes I could not understand. JZ has always told it like it is, because what she said to me and about me rang true to my ears.

If you ever want to be free, you can never deny the truth. I have always contemplated what type of gift could I give JZ in appreciation that she does not have. I contemplated that as many times as she has left her body just to let us know God is, that every time she leaves her body and Ramtha comes in, she dies. I have come to the conclusion that the only gift I can give her is that one day we end up in the same place after accomplishing the intention of living for two hundred years, and counting, and that she knows that I appreciate all that she has done.

Most of us think that all we are is what we see with our eyes, and we do not think about what is in the other ninety percent of the brain that we do not use. My understanding is that consciousness and energy create what we want and uncreate what we don't want when we apply the different methods of discipline that Ramtha has taught us. We are beginning to tap into the other ninety percent of the brain: for example, to be able to heal myself, which I have done many times; to be able to manifest into the palm of my hand coins; to be able to manifest a feather into my hand; to be able to find cards with my own symbols on a large fenced field, blindfolded; to be able to go through a huge labyrinth and find the Void at its center, without eyes; to be able to bring forth an animal that was dead back to life, little baby turkeys. These are a few of the things, for example, that I have learned. I haven't mastered them all at will but I have had the experience of doing it, making it happen. So therefore, I have created the neuronet in my brain for magic number one, to be able to learn how to do these things consistently.

And I would say the only reason why I don't do them consistently is because I am, like every other man or woman, lazy. And I am focusing on overcoming that as well, and I will. There's nothing we cannot create or uncreate. JZ Knight has proven that, as a human being like I am. And one of the greatest things I am working on is how to focus to be able to live for two hundred years without death, sickness, and disease in this body.

I chose to be a black man because in my last lifetime I was a white man with blue eyes and blond hair. I was very arrogant. My contemplation gave me the knowledge to realize that my anger and bitterness against the white race are merely because of what I was in my last lifetime. I know that I was wretched in that lifetime. I owned slaves and disliked them. I have learned from Ramtha that anything you have a prejudice against — anything that you hate — that in order to gain knowledge from that, you must live another lifetime and be exactly what you hated. The experience gives you wisdom.

So in this lifetime, I firmly believe that I made the choice — like many of you who are black — to be black because of who I was in that last lifetime and how I was so ignorant so as to hate the black race, the black culture. God gave me the greatest gift in this lifetime, to allow me to come back and experience what I hated so much, what I didn't want to be a part of, what I thought was lesser than me. What greater experience could there be than to be able to come into a lifetime and to be the exact thing that I despised, that I ruled, that I hated, that I felt I was better than? What greater opportunity could there be than to experience that same hate, the belittlement, the unworthiness, unable to have authority over anyone, unworthy to have equal pay, to put my children in the same school? What better test could God give me than to let me come back as what I hated the most, and be done with my prejudice forever?

So, white brothers and sisters, contemplate that in the last lifetime you might have been black men and women. It is a great opportunity to allow you to come back and be what you despised the most, for the great lesson is that color, race, male, and female are truly nothing but an illusion. We are all one common denominator. We all have God within us equally.

So I am proud to take responsibility at half of one hundred years old, thanks to Ramtha, for what I chose on the Plane of Bliss and my life review before coming into this life. And all of the players in my life chose to be the players so I could learn and overcome. Whatever I do, whatever I have done, whatever happens to me, I have created this lifetime with its joy and passion, its victimization and tyranny, and its lack.

When my eyes became opened and I started looking at things in this lifetime from a perspective of choice, I realized that no white man is at fault for who and what I am, for where and how I have lived, for how I am educated. I am responsible for that. Do you realize how easy it is to be the victim? Woe to victims, to black victims. Contemplate how easy it is to buy into being less-than, to always expect someone to do something for you. We are only here in these bodies and this lifetime because we deserve and need the lesson. We were not cast into these bodies and this race because we were helpless. That is more victimization.

Other cultures, other races are not separate from you. God cannot be separate from any color, from any thing. Do you think that white is better than black or that black is better than white or Mexican? Is Mexican better than Arab or Indian? You are lost in that thinking. You spend your energy blaming people, places, things, times, and events for your own creation. What about your own wisdom? Do you think anyone suffered the 9-11 incident by accident? If you have understood the earlier statement that I made about consciousness and energy creates the nature of reality, you can see that everything happens for a greater purpose and learning experience regardless of how minor or how serious it may be. I send my love and my prayers of understanding to the loved ones that lost relatives in 9-11.

I see the white man and woman, the black man and woman, the Japanese, Korean, the German, and the Jew — all races — as one, and that one is God. Behold God in every one of us, the equalness that we are. The fat, the thin, the rich, the poor, all points of prejudice are equal. How can we act like we don't see these things? How can we point a finger of blame at people, places, things, times, and events and have four fingers and a thumb pointing back at us without taking responsibility?

Love is the cosmic glue that holds everything together within this universe. I have an agreement with God in this lifetime to be what I am. Churches — Baptist, Catholic, Jehovah's Witnesses, Christians — are nothing but an illusion and a game. They have nothing to do with God, and separate classes are another illusion, a game. You choose which field you wish to play on and create in your life.

It came out in California that a couple of black churches were saying that Jesus Christ was black, and so they started painting the Last Supper with all black people around the table. That made a lot of sense to me. Why would God only be white? I even thought for years, how can we love God if he is portrayed as a blond white man? That was really puzzling, to pray to a white man and then, if you got caught outside after dark, you could be killed.

When I came to Ramtha's School of Enlightenment and saw all of these white people, I really thought I had walked into my worst nightmare because at that time I was the only black man in that audience and there were two black women, out of fifteen hundred people. And there were more women, white women, than anything else in the audience. This was back in 1988.

One of the things that freed me was when Ramtha came into the audience and said that he was mahogany-skinned with woolly hair. Well, I am looking at this white body, this beautiful blonde lady, and he is channeling through her body, and he says he is mahogany-skinned with woolly hair. Well, I knew right off no white people have woolly hair; he had to be black. And it gave me a sense of freedom because I knew he wasn't a mortal human; he was a God: Number one, he never judges you for anything that you do, have done, or will do, and you still feel a love from him regardless of all the things that you have done; the feeling is no different than when you have done nothing. The love is just as equal and as strong, and he expects for you to be responsible for all actions. I have watched flowers that are brought to him on the stage open all the way up immediately after his presence on the stage, after him smelling or touching them. I have yet to see some man, mortal human, man or woman, do that. It's the simple things, you know. I guess the greatest thing is when he talks to you or points his finger at you across the arena that's as large or larger than a football field in a group of one-thousand-plus people. You can feel the power of that finger or you can feel the power of those eyes as you have never felt it before, and you feel it all through your soul and every cell in your body. Make no mistake about it.

The day when I decided to go on the staff of Ramtha's School of Enlightenment, I was in the process of being hired and the staff was talking about how JZ was going to hire this black man. I was totally shocked because I was thinking I was coming into a spiritual school, and in my ignorance, I really thought it wouldn't even be prejudiced because we were all looking for God. I allowed myself to feel different. I felt like everybody else was better than me because they were white and I was black. So that then kept me distant from them. Still I loved the teaching and I loved the Teacher. And in my soul I felt an equality because now he was saying we were all equal because we were all God.

Well, then I became a Red Guard on the staff and they put me at the front door. That means when everybody comes into the school, I am basically the first one that they see when they walk in. One day, watching people from Germany and France and Italy and Spain and Norway and the Netherlands, when they saw me, I could really tell that they saw a greater difference than anybody else, because a lot of times they would walk in the door, but when they would see me, they would look at me from my head to my toes, like I was something they had never seen before — mainly the Germans — like they had never seen a black man close up; they had heard about them but had never seen one. And so many times they would come up to me and ask me if they could touch my hair. And they would touch my hair and they were amazed that it was so soft.

I listened to a lot of people because I am a people's person. I like to be around the people, not the in-crowd. And I would hear them say that the in-crowd always felt they were better than everybody else. So one day I decided when people started coming in the door I would say, "Greetings," and hug them, men and women. And some of them would just stiffen up like they had been touched by poison — mainly the men — but I would just hug them anyway and that broke within me the stiffness. And the more I did that, the more white people became open to me, became friendly, and wanted to talk and be around me.

Seeing everybody as a God and everybody as equal had nothing to do with the skin color. And that really freed me up from a certain amount of prejudice that I had — and fear that I had — about white people. But until then, during the eighties, I was totally militant; I hated that the white people had the upper hand over every other culture. And I could never understand a person that was what they called poor white trash not having everything they wanted, because I thought their brothers and sisters ruled the world. All they would have to do is play the game and they could get anything they wanted, although they don't always know that. So seeing everyone as a God turned each person into an individual for me.

Feeling a sense of love — and I use the word love as best I can; maybe freedom would be a better word rather than love — toward everybody made me feel a lot more comfortable myself in a lot of ways. I became more comfortable being around whites than being around blacks — and I don't quite understand that but I did — because the whites have everything and the blacks are endeavoring to keep up with the whites instead of keeping up with themselves.

The white culture as a whole has come a long way in my lifetime. I think it is split into a segment that still thinks the only perfect person is like them. But what I have learned is that in every culture you will find a certain segment of ignorant people that want to blame, the same as in the black culture that want to blame every other culture for what they don't have or what they are struggling with. But the trick of it is the white culture is not what is holding us down. It is the black culture's consciousness of two hundred years ago that is holding us down today. They cannot get over or want to forget slavery, even though who they are now was not there then.

They are holding onto a time — a people, places, things, times, and events — of two hundred years ago. But what if they found out they were not even black in their last lifetime? Maybe they were slave owners two hundred years ago. They hold onto that woe-is-me victimization, but when you look at history, you find there is not a culture in the world that has not at sometime or another been enslaved. And so it really makes me understand how ignorant we are as a people to think we are the only enslaved people in the world when there was a time when we were slave owners ourselves. The sad part about it is that even now — and I am talking about lawyers, doctors, judges, professors — there are still blacks that say, "if it were not for the white man, this or that would not be happening to us." The real truth of the matter is that we as a black culture have not taken responsibility for ourselves. And we hang onto our grandparents' and great-grandparents' experiences and what they taught us to keep holding us down today.

I had a real challenge six years ago when I went back to California to see some of my doctor and lawyer and judge and professor friends, and they are still talking about the white man in the year 2000: "If it weren't for the white man, we could do this and do that." I am sure they have had experiences in coming through college that held them back or gave them a big challenge. As I travel around the United States and watch blacks, when anything is said to them or anything is done to them, they feel somebody is being racist toward them. But the truth of the matter is that blacks themselves hold a greater prejudice than anybody on the earth, and it might just be about how people react to that chip on your shoulder. They need to understand that this racism that keeps coming back to them is only what they perpetuate by holding onto their past. So if you keep holding onto that you are lesser-than if you are black, guess what? That is all you can ever manifest in your life. What a victim.

And what a setup for a government that has programs for what they call the minority people. They say if you are a minority, you can get more, you can get in colleges, you can get certain programs and additional money. That practice keeps holding down the black people that buy into it. Black people see it as a plus when it is really a negative. If God made us all equal, why would you want to even accept a special program that makes you a victim, that you get something no one else can get because of your color? Why not just use the mind that you have — that is equal to any other mind in the world, which is the mind of God — and be a genius?

One of the things I have always been against is to get any type of aid from the government because I am a minority, because it makes you almost feel like they have to give you an extra hand because you are not good enough to meet expectations, and I resent that. I think welfare has been the worst thing that the government ever created. Now they are doing away with it. In the welfare system you have generation after generation that have been on it, and basically what they learn is that they don't have to work, they don't have to be responsible because the government will take care of them. Well, if the government doesn't even give everyone free water, something is wrong with this system.

All of these are choices. But as a kid I remember that we used to be on welfare. And we would go every Wednesday down to the food line and they would give us cheese, powdered milk, oatmeal, and beans. I always had a sense of worry about the government giving us this food, about being on the lower end of the totem pole. I always felt there could be something wrong with this food, that it was a way they could poison us. I got that when I learned how they killed the Indians by giving them diseased blankets. And of course at that time I wasn't aware how many whites were on welfare too.

I never felt bad enough in the black culture to ever join the political activities of the Black Panthers or to join the Muslims, because I felt that was a trick within itself. I saw black people that were perpetuating separation. The Islamic religious leader Louis Farrakhan talks about blacks should have their own separation from the whites. Well, separation is prejudice.

In Ramtha's School of Ancient Wisdom I learned that everybody is a God and everything we do is done by choices, and that for every one choice we make, we have ninety-nine other choices. I realized that whatever was happening to me in the moment was about whatever choice I made right now. So then I started to become very responsible for myself and stopped blaming my mother, my father, my stepfathers, white teachers, black teachers. I took responsibility for having created this life for a great lesson. And the lesson, I later learned, was because I had so much hate for black people in the last lifetime that this lifetime I had to become black to experience my hate.

Now I can honestly say that I see everybody as a God. But I do see some people as ignorant. I don't see racist people anymore as much as I see ignorance, and that racism is just about ignorance and fear.

My first three wives were black and then my fourth relationship was with a white woman that was brought up in the Mormon Church. Now she fought the concept of the Mormon Church but she still talked to blacks from that Mormon background, that they weren't good enough and what they should do with their lives. It was, "do this for me," and, "do that for me." And I said many times in that relationship, "You know, you talk to me like I am your nigger. You don't ask me; you tell me what to do." Yet, at the same time, she had a passion to be with black men, perhaps from a past life experience. She now has a son that was from a black African.

And then I had a relationship with a German woman. I realized with the first meal she fixed for my children and myself that she was coming from World War II and lack. There was very little food on the plate for my fourteen-year-old son, and when he asked for more, she said that was enough. This is a growing young man. When I cook, I cook a four-course meal of solid food. This was about her experience versus my experience, not about our color or gender.

So now I am married to a Norwegian. Of course there is a culture thing going on here too, that the only way to live is the Norwegian way, a perfect way. She is blonde and blue-eyed. She had only experienced one black person in her life, in her class in school. She never got to know him or got close to him. And when she got in college, she loved to be around black people. They gave her more of a sense of freedom. When we got to talking about our former relationships, her freest relationships had been with black men. The white men, the Norwegians, were not free.

A year after we got married, I told her I was not in love with her until I walked down the aisle. In my discipline of truth, to free myself from my own past and my own necromancers, I confessed that I unconsciously married her because of something that I had been denied in this lifetime, and that was never looking at, touching, or being with a blonde-haired woman with blue eyes. Consciously or unconsciously, I was determined to experience that. She was shocked when I told her, but I was in a moment of speaking my truth. But since then, I did fall in love with her, most definitely.

Being married to a Norwegian, it is interesting to watch just what they eat. They want pasta and fish and bagels and cream cheese. As a black man married to this white woman, it has been really interesting because I like greens, mashed potatoes, smothered chicken, or smothered porkchops, and I love cornbread. These are things my wife never even heard of. When I cooked for her, she loved it. So I came to realize more and more that prejudice between cultures is really nothing but ignorance. That is all it is. I enjoy the mixture of the cultures because I like to learn.

The power for change rests with us as a black culture and with us as individuals and our choices. Stop being a victim; stop seeing yourself as an African American, because if you do, you bring forth all of the karma that African Americans have brought on themselves for eons. Be rather a God/man, God/woman fully realized, equally. Being a God/man, God/woman realized is understanding and knowing that God exists within you — God exists in all of us, all living things — to take on the responsibility to evolve that God within us and create our life magnificent from that knowingness, to be the wholeness of all things. That applies to male and female. Don't hold onto excuses to blame the white man. I have done it; I know the game. So when you say that the white man rules the earth, I will agree with you. But what decade or century in time did you rule the earth as a black man against the whites? When did the Jews rule? When did the Indians or Arabs rule the world? All that you point the finger at now is a circle you have participated in. This is knowledge.

How many lifetimes must a woman suffer and be less than what man is because man feels superior? Do not fall into the trap of using women as a sexual tool, lest you come back as a woman. Women are learning to take back their power, just as the earth will soon recover herself when men no longer have to take from her the life force, which is her blood, the oil of the earth, and when all mankind truly understand and learn how to respect nature, because nature is our greatest teacher. And one day that will happen. The smallest blade of grass, the smallest insect, the smallest bird, the smallest creature all hold God within it, and all give back to God, in some form, rejuvenation — all but mankind. That day will come to an end and Mother Nature will be restored at all costs.

And the women learning to take back their power is when they no longer become submissive to men, and she no longer thinks that she needs men to make her whole and complete. She will no longer have to bear a child and be married and keep up with the Joneses to think she has fulfilled her life as a woman. When a woman realizes that, not intellectually, then she truly understands that she is more powerful than any man on the face of the earth naturally, because she can give birth and bring forth life and a man cannot. All things are brought to life from the female gender. Men have ruled the world for eons. Women, the female power, could rule the world soon because they are waking

I HAVE TAKEN RESPONSIBILITY FOR MY OWN CREATION

up. Honor their power or be at their mercy. Honor your sisters, your mothers, your nieces, your aunties, your daughters.

The earth is not Father Nature but Mother. All things come from Mother. I give great gratitude to my mother. Without women, we would not be here today. No man has given birth to babies, brought forth life on the earth. This is a great power of the female gender. Without men there would not be life either. Men play a great part in bringing life from their seed, their sperm, their wisdom. Men should be responsible for what they create in their life and help provide for their beloved wife and for their children. Men should also be responsible for raising children. They should be the role models of their knowledge, not some sports. The men should spend time with their children, should teach them what they know and greater, should teach them that the woman is nothing to be abused or beaten up or used because, like I said before, without the women none of us would be here today.

As you give up the power to people, places, things, times, and events — because it is easier to blame than to shoulder responsibility — you get tired of seeing others with everything you desire for yourself. Learn to blame no one. Don't waste your time judging. Get up and do whatever it takes with God's love to help you. It is hard to face what you are in this lifetime, especially if you don't like it.

Blame leads to victimization. Blame leads to drugs and alcohol, cigarettes, pills. Be stronger than that. All you have to do is the same that I have done. Give it up and go forward and clutch onto the God within you and call it forth. If you do these things you will be free. You will have more freedom than you can imagine. You will be seeing your life as free, yourself as equal to all.

I am not one looking in from the outside and trying to figure it out. I have not always taken responsibility. I have been a fool; I have been ignorant, but I am one that has walked the walk but with much greater wisdom now than some church can give me. I have tapped into the Holy Spirit within each of us — each of us — regardless of gender or race. I have gained greater knowledge from Spirit to be responsible for who and what I am. I am awake now and the victimization and tyranny are over with. I now take responsibility with love and great joy. I had to say all of this to myself before I could say it to you. I am not better or different. I am one who has realized the victim I have been; I have learned, and I regret none of it.

I have written in the past about my dyslexia. It was a perfect opportunity to be a victim and point my finger at many, many people. I blamed the white teachers that could not teach me. But I took responsibility; I beat dyslexia. And because I chose this in this lifetime, I can see that in my last lifetime I was a most astute entity. I could read and spell all things and made fun of those who could not. I actually understand that my dyslexia in this lifetime comes from so many past lifetimes of reading Hebrew and Egyptian texts, reading right to left, which is backward — dyslexic — in English. So I chose not to be able to do so in this lifetime until I made a choice of change. I made the choice to be responsible. I made a choice to become greater than what I had made fun of.

Do not condemn what I say until you do it. Once you do it, you can never condemn it, because who is more responsible for what we are than we ourselves? We are our own creation in this lifetime. Accept the responsibility, the credit for what we have created. Accept the great powers we have on this earth to help us realize our divinity, our foreverness. The easiest thing is to cast this aside and not listen, because the hardest thing is responsibility.

Do not put this idea down or make fun of it. It frightens you that this might be the truth. And it is going to be tough to face up to your truth and be more responsible. You can't wait for Jesus to save you. You must save yourself. And when you make up your mind that you are greater than your humanity, there is something within you that throws out that

RESPONSIBILITY FOR MY OWN CREATION

love ... ...ple, all places, all things, all times, and all events ... ...d within you that has total joy and no judgment again... anyone or anything.

I came onto this earth plane by myself and I will leave by myself. But nothing dies on this earth — nothing dies. In the winter months, a tree, when it looks bare and dead, is dreaming the dream of spring. And it knows that nothing ever dies.

When I say that you created who and what you are, that you are responsible for your life — you may be a drug addict, a gay man or woman, you may be black or white, Jewish or Caucasian — I mean that you chose this experience in this lifetime. You most likely experienced the opposite in your last lifetime and came back as what you hated for the sake of understanding it and retiring that emotional storm into wisdom.

How much power do you desire to give away to those you feel are greater than you? Those who rule are not greater. They do not have your power. If you combine your consciousness with theirs, you empower them. When you buy into the consciousness that you are equal to them, they can no longer be empowered by your acceptance. Yes, slavery happened, but we agreed to the consciousness that let it happen. Perhaps we had been enslavers in another lifetime or needed that experience so its wisdom would empower us beyond measure in a future generation.

If you are black you have less if that is your desire, but if you desire to have greater, you can have greater. And only the consciousness of thinking someone is better than you will allow that consciousness to thrive, because you are what you think, and you manifest it daily in your life just as I did. When you first read my story, you may pity me because I had it so rough. But when you realize what I have realized, you will see that I created it all for a greater lesson in this lifetime.

Be who you really are. This does not mean you have to be separate from the white race. Separation allows one to think they are better than the other and promotes prejudice.

Ramtha is the only one in my lifetime who was ever brave

enough to tell me the truth, whether I liked it or not. But because I chose him as my Teacher, I accepted all that he said and made a choice to change. My heart now is so filled with the love of God that no one and nothing can make me feel less than them.

I have honestly told you my truth, spoken to you what I have learned in my own experience. My intent is to share truth with you. And I feel that no one is to blame for my life, for what I am. I have lived for myself and I honor the choices I have made. If I had to do it all again, I would do it no other way than the way I have done it this time because I love who and what I am today and the peace that I have gained within myself.

Becoming: What I mean when I say becoming is we all have a greater consciousness within us. That's why we are here on this earth today, to fulfill that unfinished business of what we came back to this earth to become. In order to do that, we must contemplate what we are, who we are, how do we treat people around us, and to know every time you judge someone, you are merely judging yourself. As I was told one day, every time you point the finger at somebody, you have three pointing back at you. Try it. You actually have three pointing back at you and your thumb, and all people that come into your life are just merely a reflection of you. And so the ones that you dislike the most are merely an example of what you are, what you don't like about yourself the most. That is the reason why they push your buttons so much and a lot of times you cannot stand to be around them. But the truth of the matter is you are seeing yourself, and this individual or individuals are merely nothing but a mirror of yourself. Sure, sometimes that can be really tough, because you judge somebody and the first thing you say is that you would never do that yourself. And the truth of the matter is that you do do that or you have done that and you are so red in the rainbow you can see every other color but red, which represents yourself; you can't see yourself.

CHAPTER THREE
When You See Everyone As Equal,
You Become Free

our dream is to be free

"You know, our dream is to be free, people — free. Free, that is the ulterior motive. That should be the motive, freedom. Freedom from what? Having to use anyone, any person, place, thing, time, or event to become it. Just to be it."

"Why do we want freedom? Because we want to own this plane and we want to own the rapacious attitudes that seem to go along with culture. We want to own those to where we have none of them inside of us because we have a mission to do, to make known the unknown. We are voyagers to Infinite Unknown."

"What kind of God would I be teaching you about if the only end to this life that you could see was a life lived like ordinary people in sort of a mundane situation that had no challenge to it and had no adversity to it and had no growth in it, to where every neighbor is trying to protect his or her own? I mean, is that the highest pinnacle of a life's achievement? The highest pinnacle is to address the adversity in life that we are vulnerable to and indeed to make short-order of it, because we do not want to be attached to it. If we are attached to it in any sort of prejudice, we are going to be tied in at that moment of weighing ourselves in the light."

— Ramtha

Seeing everyone as equal is finding the neutral point. Who would we be and how would we think if we were raceless, if we were no race at all?

I had a great conversation with a young woman friend of mine named Tiffany who endeavors to experience that very thing. For much of her life, she had not contemplated why she chose a white mother and a black father. But she later realized that it was because she didn't want to be either. She wanted to be neutral. Her perception was that the whites hated her because of her black physical ability, and the blacks hated her because she looked white. She eventually became more comfortable with blacks than with whites because they were more accepting of diversity. I think blacks tend to see themselves as victims and they welcome another victim. She was more comfortable with the black women because she saw herself as a victim.

Tiffany has a father that is still, after all of these years, hung up on all of his racism. I got the impression when I had the chance to interview him that it was all about the hate that he had for blacks and how important he wanted to be as a black. If that were not true, he would not be living in a town where he is the only black man in the whole town. He avoids blacks and lives in a white community — most of them younger than him — where he can put them down and always show them how he is better than other blacks. There are no other blacks around to prove him wrong. So he is a perfect example of self-perpetuation.

When I went to West Africa in the early eighties, I found out from the African people that they have such a great resentment toward the black Americans. They tried to make the black African Americans feel responsible and obligated to the Africans still in Africa, because they feel that we sold them out and came to America. They would say to me, "You owe us." And even within the black cultures in Africa, with different tribes amongst themselves, it is black culture fighting black culture. It is no different than here, or Irish Catholic against Irish Protestant, or Vietnamese against Vietcong, Muslim against Christian, Arab against Jew, Middle Eastern against Westerners.

These people are holding onto so much of their pasts that it makes it difficult for them to make a difference today in their own lives. They hang onto the things that keep them from being free so they don't have to change, so they don't have to make changes in their lives. I hope people will read this and it will turn on a switch, that they will be able to say "that is me." I want them to see "he was this and now he is that." Or they will see people who are still being enslaved by their own thoughts and they don't realize it.

Here is some of what the young woman I interviewed had to say about her perspective on prejudice between the races. I interviewed her because she chose to have a white mother and a black father yet chose neither race for herself. She chose to be neutral. This is her journey to freedom, to seeing everyone — and herself — as equal:

Sir Robert: Can you tell us a little about your family, your background, and yourself?

Tiffany: My ethnic origin is Jamaican, Navajo Indian, Chinese, Irish, and that is from my father's side. But you wouldn't know that because he is very dark-skinned. My mother is French, Irish, and Scottish.

I always saw my mother for my mother and I always saw my father as my father. I didn't see color. It wasn't until I got into school that I found I had a natural affiliation to black girls. One day when I came home, my mother said, "Stop acting like you are black; stop acting like a black girl," and this was confusing to me. I didn't even have the words to articulate, "But, Mom, what are you talking about?" She didn't want me to be black. Here she was in love with a black man, but there was still a part of her that didn't want me to be black. And yet, what do you want me to do? On my cellular level my genetics show that I am fifty percent black and fifty percent white. What am I supposed to do?

To me, I loved hanging out with the black girls because they danced; they were into music. I love that. I have always been attracted to music. Dancing is my thing. And white people to me were stiff; they were boring; they were pretentious. They didn't have a clue.

So this set the premise for my whole life. I dated only black men. Although they were bullshitters and con artists — which I knew they were going to, you know, be obnoxious — but, see, black men are very forthcoming. I mean, they are just like, "You know what? You are fine. I want to date you," or "What's your number?" whereas the white man is way more subtle.

My biggest realization was while I was in school; I was a mixed person. I got prejudice from the black people because I had good hair. "You just want to be white." I am like eleven, ten, twelve years old. I don't know what I want to be. I just want to be free. I have no definition, so to speak, you know? I don't fit anywhere yet. And yet there were the dark-skinned women and men that already said, "Well, you want to be white."

I was articulate; I was smart; I did very well in school. I participated. I was a cheerleader. I did all the sports. My father was an amazing athlete and I inherited that genetically. And so here I was participating in it all, and I would get conflict from black women. "You are just trying to be white. You are denying your black heritage." And I was in confusion. I would say, "What do you mean? I am just being me. I am just being Tiffany. I am not trying to be black or white." But I was always more socially acceptable than they were, so they competed.

There is this woman thing of competition and then there is the racial thing.

So it is like I know I took it all on because white girls didn't accept me because I wasn't white, but they loved me because I was captain for three years in cheerleading and I was the captain of all the dance groups I have ever been in. I had that strength to do it and I had the rhythm to do the dance. But there was always that jealousy or something.

At that time I was ignorant. I didn't know. I only knew insecurity and why doesn't everybody like me, or what is going on. And then there were the black girls rejecting me because I had nice hair and perhaps, you know, there were the black guys that liked me. And I was even insecure in that; I didn't even know that.

So it isn't until now I realize you have the white attitudes, the racial white thing going on, and then you have that black thing going on, so you have conflict. You truly have conflict at the cellular level. And what I mean by that is that what I have learned, with your basic physics, is that every attitude is laid down and held into a neuronet. And this is the job of the brain. The brain holds it because it is holding a pattern based on "I might need to know this for future reference, so I am going to hold onto it." It is the computer that records all information; this is the brain.

And so I can say that from a cellular level I see myself as a mixed person when I am walking down the street. I have black and white genetics and I walk down the street and I see a white woman with a black man, and I go, "She doesn't understand him," or I have resentment toward her because she is with him. Here I have a white mother but yet I hate white people. What is that all about?

So there was a lot of conflict going on inside myself about what do I do. Who am I? And it wasn't until I really got into Ramtha's School of Enlightenment and the spiritual journey and realizing I am really neither black nor white did it bring it up. I realized that I wasn't any of these things and then I really began to love the adversity of having a white mother and a black father and everything that my father had contributed to my life.

I want to be neutral. I contemplate this because I love — I love — I love being black and I love being white because I get to go into a community and I get to experience something that a black person that doesn't have any white heritage doesn't get to experience. And not only that, I get to be special. I mean, I have nothing but cousins that have blond hair and blue eyes. I walk in and it's really obvious that I do not have blond hair and blue eyes, okay? And then I get to walk into my family. My father is dark. And I have very dark-skinned people in my family, and then I have some light-skinned, but even the lightest-skinned person is darker than I am. So it is still obvious that I am different. I get to experience both sides and I love that. I get to look at all of my attitudes but it is still about being neutral. It is about you know what? I am neither one of these things and I am everything.

I think as a child, your father and your mother represent the world to you. And so how you relate to a man is how your father related to you. How you relate to a woman is how your mother related to you. My mother was always my confidante, my sister, my friend, so we were very close. But in a cultural sense, she was white. So when I came across black girls that were very outspoken and held nothing back, it intimidated me; I was afraid. And they would say things to me I quite frankly just didn't know how to respond to because we didn't talk about those things. In my mother's family, those things were kept under the carpet. We kept up the front. Everybody stayed happy, and even though we weren't really happy, we pretended we were and there wasn't that directness.

And then all of a sudden I get into junior high school and high school, and there are the layers of all this stuff that race has to go through. But then these black women, they just let it all out. I would witness black girls cursing out their boyfriends,

I mean, cursing them out royally for looking at another woman or something. And I thought, wow, that's crazy. I would have never done that because that is not acceptable. You have to be demure and reserved and quiet and all these things because he's got to like you. You know, there are so many layers there.

And then I finally realized I have both of these qualities. I have that directness and that outrageousness and I also have that reservation. And it has been a trip; it really has. I mean someone who is bringing in a child that is of mixed cultures and it is black or white or mixed cultures, whatever race it is, there is a lot to contemplate because you want to acknowledge this being's coming in as something that is beyond the race and the color and the gender. But you also have to be willing to acknowledge that that is also going to be present.

And that is the same thing that Ramtha, our Teacher, has been telling us. You know, it really is outrageous when he comes back not only just through a white, blonde-haired, blue-eyed lady's body — which is his second lifetime — but then he is black and tall, so he is neither. He is not white or black. He is a God. And to me that is just so deep and so heavy. And in the same token you can realize why black people have such a problem with Ramtha, because most black people would say why didn't you come through a black woman or a black man, which he is. Why did he choose a white woman? I see it as that he is endeavoring to send a message.

And as Ramtha has said many times, racism is over with. This is over with; give it up. And we shouldn't teach our children, our grandchildren about racism anymore because this is in the past. This is history. This drama is over with. We have to look a lot further than our lives to still hang onto something that happened two hundred years ago, which when you really think about it, it is really nothing really special because the Jews were slaves, the Germans have been slaves, the whites have been slaves. We all have played this game of being rulers over other cultures.

And it is not to say I don't understand the plight. But I also want to say that let's acknowledge and love the culture. I mean, I love the culture and I don't even really know that much about my black heritage, and my father being Jamaican, I don't know as much as I would like to know about the Jamaican heritage. I mean, I have never even been to Jamaica. I have never even met my grandfather. I would love to know about that and take my son to Jamaica.

Just honor, respect, and love the heritage that you are. But it is not really who you are. It is what you are experiencing in the moment, you know? I also want to say my family is French, Irish, and Scottish. I mean, I can also go to Europe and experience that, and honor and respect that, you know, and love that and teach that to my son.

And so it is not slamming one or the other or saying that you have to forget about being black. It is just that; Be proud of being black. But you also don't have to hold onto the anger as if you are special because it is going to make you somebody. You are already somebody; just by the fact that you were born today, you are somebody. You are worth being acknowledged because you took on the path of a human being. And you obviously are here for mastery of something, whatever it is on the various degrees of that. And that is worthy.

As Tiffany points out, that freedom comes from not blaming anyone else for your life, not being a victim. To me, freedom is not about being the corporate person, not being the failure in life, not being perfection, because perfection is itself a limitation. To me, being free is allowing your thoughts to flow, not being a victim of your own mind. Freedom is to allow everyone to be and do whatever they desire to be and do, with no judgment. Let them fulfill their mandate they came to this earth to fulfill. Give everyone the freedom to speak and think however they desire, including your children. Don't make them live by our mandate.

Does that mean to let them be wild and crazy, outrageous and disrespectful? Wild and crazy, outrageous and unique, yes, but disrespectful, no. Whatever they create — whatever we create — in this lifetime that is disrespectful, we are in error because all people are equal to what we are. Our perception is nothing but that: a perception, a point of view.

Freedom is to be. Our children came back to experience everything they desire to be. They need to be free and know. Everyone and everything that you magnetize into your life is there because they are more of what you really are or they are the great battle that you are fighting to clear up, eliminate, and change in yourself. Either way, we are talking about freedom.

We should have the freedom to hold any opinion about anything without judgment. My opinion and your opinion and their opinion may be different. So when I say to be free is to not judge, it sets you free as well. Freedom is key to growth in life. In order to love someone else, you first have to love who and what you are yourself. So be free, not to be crazy, but to be yourself allowed.

Freedom is not controlling my lady, being a tyrant, or a bully. Freedom is allowing her to have her free will to do and say and act any way she so desires. Freedom is not to compare what is appropriate. Freedom has no boundaries. Freedom does not just fit in our box. It allows everyone's choices for themselves.

Freedom does not make another feel guilty or make them feel blame or make them feel sorry or make them feel responsible. Freedom is allowing. If you react to what they do or say, you are not allowing but trying to control them and make them fit your own ideas. It is about when you point the finger at someone else, you are merely seeing your own reflection. And when you see your own reflection, it makes you angry. That is what you have to deal with in order to become free. When you put a judgment on anyone, that is what you have to deal with, to allow another to say or do whatever they desire without becoming a victim of it. Why would you become emotional about it? Why would you become angry about it?

The freedom that I speak about is understanding truly that what a person says or does, does not affect you. That is freedom. As long as we choose to be affected, we are not free. We are victims and we are blaming others. Anytime someone does something that you do not like and you have a judgment on it, you are truly looking at yourself. Then you are locked into a box. You think it has nothing to do with you, but because you are so involved in it, it has everything to do with you.

When you can allow everyone, every race, every creed, every color to do whatever they desire to do, you begin to be free. But if you see a white man doing what he desires to do and you judge him, you are judging yourself. You are not being free when you judge the white woman for doing whatever she wants to do. And if what they say and what they do makes you feel bad or sad, then you are being a victim.

If you see another black man do something that you feel threatened by, once again, it is merely your reflection and you are the victim. You are not allowing yourself to be free. Your buttons are being pushed because you see a reflection of yourself in what they are saying, what they do, how they look, how they walk or talk. An attitude of freedom is what allows women to be equal to men and men to women, to speak their minds regardless of what men or other women or other races think.

The key to freedom is not judging people, places, things, times, and events but to allow everyone to be who and what they are, to see their moments of life as they want them to be. Don't be so quick to change the illusion. Freedom is allowing, because we all have a greater destiny. We all have to see our injustice in the light, and we have to experience it once again in another lifetime.

So all of the judgment I have had against white people is because they pushed my buttons. All the judgment I have had against Mexican people is because they have made me look at how I am and what I am. And I didn't like what I saw, so I became angry. These days I realize that a lot of what I have seen and allowed to push my buttons is what I have been or what I am now.

The remedy is to let them say what they want to say, do what they want to do. Don't have any emotions about it. Be free from it, because when you can become the Observer of it is when you become truly free. Being the Observer is harder than being involved in it. When you are involved in it, you can deny that you see yourself in other people. "That's not me," you say. "That is you. I wouldn't do that. You are just saying that." But when you observe, you have nothing to say. You quietly within you change it or you quietly within you continue it. That to me is being free.

Those of us who are tyrants and victims, I truly believe that if we don't take a grip on our lives — take responsibility for our lives — all we will do is come back and experience it again and again and again until we take responsibility for who and what we are. That includes loving everyone and everything, because you must ask what it is in someone you don't love that you cannot love about yourself. And I am not talking about physical love. I am talking about love for God that exists in every living thing, from a worm to a tree to a butterfly. When we reach a level of being able to do that, we are free, with no judgments — free.

If the different races and religions of the world respected each other in freedom, conflicts like we are seeing all over the world today — in Kosovo, Afghanistan, Pakistan, India, the terrorist attack of 9-11, Iraq, Northern Ireland, South Africa

— would not be happening now. If we researched all the sides of the history of these conflicts with an open mind, we would find out that it isn't what it looks like and that in the end we are all human beings searching for the same goal — freedom; we would have a different understanding and position about what is really happening. You can only arrive at this vista, though, if you have an open mind and the willingness to study the history of all the parties involved.

Let's not continue to have anger and hate from the past and let's start anew. After all, we cannot change what has happened. We can only change our choices in the present and be more intelligent and more open for change for the betterment of all people. If it is true that we were created in the image of God, if we are not merely the accident of meaningless random evolution but the result of a cohesive, observable intelligence, as the latest discoveries in quantum physics show experimentally, then all humans should have the right to have their own religion, their own belief, their own desire, have their own land to harvest and provide nourishment for their families without the threatening cloud of fear, insecurity, and shame looming on the horizon. So once again, in the end, it all goes back to that basic right of freedom for all people, the necessary ingredient that impregnates the ground and makes it fertile with new life.

Are we saying that being free means you may take my home because I don't believe in your religion? Hell, no. Don't you have a home of your own? I don't want your home. I don't want to take anything from you. But I will defend my right to protect the home I, myself, have created in freedom. I desire for all people to live and share this right equally, because if you feel you have a right to my home, then that would mean that you think I am lesser than you, wouldn't it? Where is the equality in that? There is none. But there is equality in allowing you to have your home, your belief, your religion, your traditions that celebrate life and freedom, as well as me having my own. The immortal words of Chief Seattle resound today with great clarity and power across the fields of time:

> "Your religion was written upon tablets of stone by the iron finger of your God so that you could not forget. The red man could never comprehend or remember it. Our religion is the traditions of our ancestors — the dreams of our old men, given them in solemn hours of the night by the Great Spirit; and the visions of our sachems, and is written in the hearts of our people."

> "Man did not weave the web of life — he is merely a strand in it. Whatever he does to the web, he does to himself."

If what I have said applies to you, don't be ashamed of it. Don't turn your back on it. Don't regret it, don't hate it, and don't hate me. All I am going to do is love you for who and what you are. If I said things that push your buttons, you know I am on the right track. Anything that did not push your buttons, you are already on the right track.

As I talk to you, I am teaching myself true love. I am not perfect. I am on this path to truly learn, and I can learn from the youngest to the oldest, from the darkest to the lightest. I have learned not to hold any prejudice. That is the only way that I can go home to my God.

It is a tough task. I might, at the present time, slip sometimes and get angry when someone points something out to me that I don't want to look at. But I am consistently working on that, every day, every word, every moment of my life, to change it. As long as you do that, you are on the pathway to the kingdom of heaven.

You may judge me, but you will get nothing but love in

return, because my journey is about satisfying my God that sees I am worthy of the kingdom of heaven and of choosing a magnificent life.

CHAPTER FOUR
How Blacks Perpetuate Prejudice Upon Themselves: Light-Skinned and Dark-Skinned Blacks

experiences that you need complete

"You came here, through a line that you created on the Plane of Bliss, to learn not what was already here but what could be here. And you came here to have something to bring up and to remind you of the experiences that you need to complete — and they can be completed as simply as you wish or as arduously as you wish — and then from that be utterly and totally free to incorporate what you have already created: an unimaginable beauty. I promise you, no one ever goes backwards when they are free of their encumbrances. They are truly liberated. They are liberated from their animal. They are liberated from their suffering. They become whole. They find the self, that which they really are."

— Ramtha

Once we were considered African Americans, then we were considered colored, then we were considered Negroes, then we were considered black. Then if anybody would call you a Negro, other than another black person, you would want to fight. And then we accepted the name African American, black man or black woman. We could call one another this, but then when another culture called us this, we would want to fight again.

Now the new name that I would like to see introduced is mahogany people, mahogany people with woolly hair; that would be a new term. Let's see where that goes and how that is accepted. But, you know, when you really think about it, all of these names are nothing but names. The bottom line to the name that we all have, regardless of our race, creeds, and colors that we are, is that we are all God/woman and God/man endeavoring to wake up, which is a rainbow of colors. And I have never, ever been more proud of my color in my life — never, ever before in my life — because now I know I chose this color, I chose this male body, I chose my eyes, and I chose my parents. And so this day I am so proud of who and what I am.

I have no prejudice against anyone. I still may have prejudice against time, places, events, but I do not have any prejudice against people. I am working on my prejudice against times, events, and places because my greatest desire is to have no judgment or prejudice on anything — on anything whatsoever — to allow everyone to see who and what they are just the way they see it, because, you know, we will only see what we want to see. We will only hear what we want to hear. But I desire for us to be able to accept and be open for change — thank God, change — that the world one day will see us all as equal, that it will make no difference what your color may be or what culture you come from, that you are equal.

And I say to you, it takes big balls and big ovaries to say that I am God/man awakening; I am God/woman awakening. Many churches will say that is blasphemy. But I say to you that is only a fact. That is what is happening in the world today. I say to you that that will be the new religion in the twenty-first and twenty-second and twenty-third centuries, is God's men and women fully realized and opening up the other ninety percent of the brain that they have never tapped into. Ignorance is forgivable, but once you gain the knowledge, you are held responsible for still being ignorant, regardless if you believe it or not. And I know that we are all equal. And in my lifetime I realize that all I had any juice on, from the white man to the light-skinned child to the white woman, that my God and I have created a whole journey so that I can own all of that prejudice and love everyone equally.

I know now that I have never been a black American before and I know I was not sold by whites as a slave and brought here from Africa. I know I am from another place and this is my first lifetime being a black American. And I know why I became a black American, because in my last lifetime, I firmly believe that I was Jewish and I had such a hate for blacks. And in reincarnating lifetimes, we always come back to deal with what we hated in the last lifetime. And in this lifetime I realize that I watched my mother working for white people and going through the back door, and we never were allowed to go through anything but the back door. Now this is in the fifties I am talking about. And watching the different TV shows and watching all of the racism in the fifties, it is something that I learned. My stepfather, who was very light-skinned and almost looked white, he hated white people. And I learned a lot from him.

I was prejudiced most of my life against light-skinned

black people. Some of them you couldn't tell from whites if you just glanced at them. Some of them had green eyes, black hair, and skin so light you couldn't tell if they were white or black. I also used to look at myself and see my dark skin. I wondered why I had dark skin while there were other black people with light skin and straight hair while I had curly, woolly hair.

My prejudice toward them was that I felt that most of the time they could "get by" in life, get jobs because they looked more like a white person versus an obvious black man or woman. Some resentment came up because of how they looked. They could play either role. They could be a white man, to their advantage, or they could be a black man, to their advantage. It is really unique to have the opportunity to do that, but I was ignorant and I was young. I didn't understand any better.

I saw what a big difference it made to a white man toward a light-skinned person. Many times I knew of light-skinned men and women who would not affiliate with the dark-skinned person because it would give away who they were; in those days, blacks and whites did not socialize. So the only socializing by light-skinned with dark-skinned was when it did not threaten their jobs.

If I did not pass the color test — and the color test is a black man or a black woman that looks so much like they were white with brown hair, maybe green eyes, could not pass necessarily for a black man but could pass for a white man or woman — because I was dark-brown-skinned with woolly, black hair and black/brownish eyes, there was no way I could pass that I was white. So in the black culture, I had a sense of prejudice against the light black man and woman.

Also there is prejudice against the dark-skinned black man from the light-skinned black man because they always thought they were better. There are some black men with light skin and greenish or brownish eyes and slick black or curly, not woolly, hair. Most of those I knew took every opportunity to pass for white. If you could get by as a white man, you had more opportunities. And when the white man wasn't looking, you snuck back home to your brothers and sisters.

And what about the prejudice against the black woman from the black man? What about the prejudice of a black man who sees the black woman as less-than? In most cases, the black man is prejudiced because the woman has an opportunity to sleep with the white master or the white man; it made her better than the black man. The black women are the greatest lovers, and so white men crave black women. Black women know how to take care of a man and how to love them, how to do for them, how to please them. And so I resented any black woman that would be with a white man. They were being taken care of and living better, and I felt they were turning their backs on the black men for a better life with a white man. A black man could not afford to give them that better life.

My prejudice for black women was small because most of my life I was raised by nothing but women: my mother, my grandmother, and my aunties and sisters. After a while I understood them, and I respected them highly because they stuck by me. At a very young age I realized the power that a black woman had. She even had the power to sleep with a white man and save a lot of her family. The black woman is so powerful that even the black man becomes submissive to the black woman.

I eventually came into a more profound relationship when one of my stepfathers was very light-skinned. I really resented him. But I have some beautiful sisters with green eyes and reddish hair, and brown hair and black eyes, that could pass for white any day. I loved them greatly, so it was interesting that I never felt a prejudice against my sisters; it was usually for men.

In some cases I felt resentment for young girls I was dating who, when we were around blacks, would be glad to hold your hand. But when they were around whites, they would act like they were white. When I look at it today, I see that they were merely into the same thing that I was into, a survival mode. I cannot blame them today. They did what they had to do. But I have to admit that I was prejudiced.

In the world today, many dark-skinned black people are prejudiced against the light-skinned, and many light-skinned black people are prejudiced against dark-skinned black people. Ignorance, a lack of knowledge, is what causes such prejudice. When you are ignorant about a culture — even your own — about how they live, how they eat, how they sleep, how they dress, how they play, what they look like, it separates you from them. That is a less than righteous path. As my wife told me one day, the bottom of my feet are just as white as her feet. I had never thought about that. She made me look at it. She said, "You are white and you are black." It is true. In most cases, your feet could pass as white.

Learning who you are and taking responsibility for who and what you are in this lifetime is so powerful. You are taking back all of your power when you see everyone as the same as what you are. When you see the light-skinned black man and the light-skinned black woman as the same as the dark-skinned, that the only thing different is that we made different choices on the color of our skin, the type of hair we had — right to the light-skinned, blond-haired black people with green eyes — you realize that difference is an illusion.

I met with a woman doctor named Jewel who is originally from Detroit. The Doctor, as she is known professionally, originally came to talk with me about prejudice against blacks. But during our conversation, she spoke a lot about gender bias and class restrictions; her own, as well as what she sees in those around her. She was motivated to become a gynecologist when she saw that her instructors in medical school withheld information from their female patients and made decisions on their behalf. Dr. Jewel felt that women needed access to a medical professional who would treat them as equals. Here is what she had to say:

Dr. Jewel: I was born in the basement of Henry Ford Hospital in Detroit, Michigan, in 1948. As I was told by my mother, African-American women had to labor in the basement as opposed to the main obstetrical department where white women could labor. So I was born in the basement of a hospital of which, thirty years later, I wound up being the first African-American woman accepted to the Department of Obstetrics and Gynecology as a staff individual.

I had no idea that gynecology was a male-dominated, male-suppressed specialty for a group of men that did not love nature, that did not love feminine energy, to be able to control the creative principle. So as I studied with gynecologists who withheld information about a woman's body from the woman, who intentionally used the information they had about a woman's body to put themselves in a superiority relationship with women, who also used the information to control creativity — to control who came to this life, who didn't come to this life, under what circumstances they would come to this life — I recognized that the woman had to have a support person, a friend in medicine that could, first of all, reempower her to who she was, that would give her creative capacity back to her, and that would protect her from an awareness that wanted to control her at their whim and, if needed, that would sterilize her at the drop of a hat, if she would not comply to their wishes.

So that was the first time in my life that I recognized that racism now moved beyond just color but it also moved into gender and that now we were looking at power: who could control what was coming into this life, who could control the vehicle that was responsible for manifesting the new life coming in.

So I had no intention at all of going into gynecology because, as most women could tell you, the most unsafe and distrustful relationship you could experience is with another woman. So I recognized this willingness to be self against self had also been initiated by men because this is based on a divide-and-conquer mentality. If women could be pitted against other women — color, length of hair, size of waist, financial status — then men could easily step in to use the gateway, the uterus, to precipitate what they wanted to have in this life, with the woman being totally ignorant that she was being used, because she was still down here dealing with whose eyelashes were the longest, not recognizing that it was not ever about any of that but about being used and controlled.

So I recognized this, and I still had to deal with women who thought they were superior to me because they had white skin or because they had blonde hair or because they had more money, not recognizing that to the warmongers and to the powerbrokers it was about "How could I use you to bring forth my intent, my desires? And if I can't use you to bring forth my intent, who gives a damn about your body or your white skin and your long eyelashes, because we will give you a hysterectomy immediately." And it amazed me how many women didn't want to accept this truth. So there are billions of hysterectomized women walking around thinking that they received good medical care, thinking that their uterus was really a problem, when all of the time it was a belief system that they bought into because they did not know who they were, that they would rather submit to a man who didn't care anything about them even though he came out of their uterus. They would rather give up the capacity to create than to know and stand for truth.

So I recognized that what I was really being asked to do was to become a protector of the uterus, not from the perspective that I was to actually evict them from the operating rooms — from having hysterectomies — but to reactivate and to reeducate their awareness of who they were. Because none of these women were going to recognize that they were the gateway for new life to come into the world.

So I recognized that standing up as a patron to the woman so that she would be respected — so that she would not be seen as a carrier of syphilis, a carrier of AIDS, without recognizing her as the mother of civilization — I realized I was actually standing at a political, social, and financial power play that took me into a whole different arena.

So I recognized that first of all I had to reinforce myself. And, secondly, I had to try to find out if I could actually draw to myself any female allies, and the last eight years of my life have been recognizing that disparity. I had no idea that so many women had been programmed to work antagonistically to themselves. So they cry about why they see their children sent to prison for life. They cry about why they see their children on drugs. They cry about not understanding why their children are mutilating themselves. They have no idea that all of this is a reflection and a ramification of their thoughts that have an effect on the fruit of their wombs, that reflect their children's choice of DNA that carries out as this behavior.

So I am saying that in the libraries of the world, in the Vatican, in the Pentagon, and in many think tanks throughout this country, the research has been done, the neurological manipulation has been implemented on a social level, through Madison Avenue, through the television, through the radio, to ensure that the mind of the woman is usurped and confiscated for the desires of those that would actually manipulate the life force of humankind.

And women still to this day are defiant about being willing to accept this truth. So one of my greatest crusades right now is to place myself in a sovereign position, which is basically to have financial freedom, so that I can write about it, that I can go forth and teach, so that I can be the example of a woman who recognizes that she is the gateway responsible for bringing forth new life into the world, so that I do not have to be subjected to the self-hate, the discrimination, and the unlovingness that so many women around the world have toward themselves.

So it is not only just a black and white issue. It is not only just a male and female issue. It is an issue, as I understand it at this point in time, of how women have been totally blinded and are totally ignorant to the fact that they are the right hand of God the Creator bringing forth life. So I am saying that I didn't have any support and recognition, that not only was it the white man that I had to deal with but, beyond him, it is his mother that is the issue. It is the woman that is the issue, that she is not willing to accept the fact that she is the gateway. Whatever she thinks and whatever she believes in she transmits that into whatever she creates, and then that unfolds into having free will in this life, that every being, plant, animal, seed has to bend to it.

Did I have any idea that gynecology was going to take me here? Of course not. When I went into gynecology, I saw that every black woman was accused of being a carrier of syphilis and gonorrhea and that the Caucasian woman was not, and that she could be reeking pus out of her vagina but white men said that it was something else going on. If a black woman came to the hospital complaining of pelvic pain, it was assumed to be nothing other than gonorrhea or syphilis. So I said where can a black woman be befriended by an individual who would not see her as a social scorn, except by me?

Now I did not go to med school to become a gynecologist. I went to it to become a neurosurgeon. But when I recognized that my colleagues knew nothing about the range of this field, I had to look further for something that was comfortable for me. And I truly did not want to become a gynecologist because my experience with women was their distrust, their backbiting, their gossiping, their competition. Did I want to basically associate with that? Of course not.

But I recognized that the men who were gynecologists did not have the best interests of women in mind. So for men to make assumptions about how my body worked, that is all they were, assumptions. But I saw from the response of women patients that their assumptions were often totally incorrect. So who could be a better gynecologist than another woman? So the call was to become a gynecologist. And if I was really to be of service, then I had to honor the call.

I had no idea that going into gynecology was going to help me become much more supportive and to become a friend to myself as a woman. Believe it or not, women are raised not to be their own best friends because so many women have already been programmed pro-men. So the mother raises the daughters to be pro-men, not pro- another woman, not pro- the gateway to human life, not pro-creator but pro-men. And that is why these religious and political organizations that have demonstrated over and over again that they behead women are still run by women. Women are raised up that regardless of what the outcome is, you are to support this; if you don't, you have no worth and that is defiling. When a woman recognizes that she is supporting something that is totally beheading her and destroying her children and she still stands for it a hundred percent, what would make her do that? She has never been given a future; she has never been given insight; she has never been given any type of vision that it could be any other way. And she has totally been blinded to the fact that she as the gateway could create and contribute something new, something different.

I was not pro Gloria Steinem in the sixties, who worked tirelessly to promote equality of pay between men and women, fought against the sexual exploitation of women, and wrote many books including the *Revolution from Within: A Book of Self-Esteem* in 1992. I had no idea what they were talking about because the black women have always been independent and had to basically get out and work to make the family work.

When a commitment is made between a man and a woman to come together, it is not for the woman to take on a man's role and it is not for a man to expect that he is exonerated from being the guardian and the director of the education that comes down through the woman to the children. So few men are able to get that, and so few women are able to recognize that.

This is still a real big thing to swallow for most women because the only paradigm that women have ever been given as an example of how you do anything has always been through the male model. So the idea of being able to use mind, to be able to use inner vision, to be able to use discipline on staying focused on that inner vision, is totally beyond what most women understand the feminine principle is really about.

I have now concluded that when we view the issue as a struggle between black and white or between male and female, it really acts like a smoke screen that keeps us from seeing the real underlying issue: a battle between recognizing ourselves as a creative mind or a sensual body, between godliness and ungodliness. If you are constantly dealing with this little bickering down here about gender and color and money, you are missing the point that the real battle is about law, order, and control versus godliness and creativity. Most people are not even seeing this. When we consider that we are all Gods and Goddesses responsible for creating our own life through our choices and our perception of the world, it moves the level of discrimination to a real serious level. The question can then be viewed in terms of, "Are you going to be a divine, free, creative agent or a spiritual slave?"

As Dr. Jewel points out, so often prejudice is against women or against race, and sometimes within gender and within race. So I say to you, brothers and sisters, a light-skinned brother to a dark-skinned brother has not taken anything from you. I say to the dark-skinned brothers and sisters, light-skinned sisters and brothers have not taken anything from you. We are still all equal. I say to the black sisters and brothers and to the light-skinned black sisters and brothers that the white man and the Mexicans and the Indians and the Jews and the Germans and the Arabs and the Norwegians and the Scots have taken nothing from us. We have all done what we have done to ourselves. We are our biggest enemy within ourselves. We are our greatest enemy.

When you look at that, you realize that nothing can continue to perpetuate slavery. If we accept slavery as truth, we then continue to perpetuate it within our lifetime. If we pass down to our children in our DNA that anyone is better than us, then the children will start saying that they are less than and that other people are better than us. And surely the white culture has passed down some of the same genetic codes by saying they are better than the blacks. So the combination of the blacks and the whites with the same inherited attitude is perpetuating continuous separation and slavery amongst one another, only to find out that perhaps the only reason you are white in this lifetime is because you were black in the last lifetime. And all that you put on the black folks in the last lifetime, you have to experience it being a white person in this lifetime. And those of you who are black in this lifetime were probably white in the last lifetime. And all that you put on black folks in the last lifetime, you have come back to be black to experience it in this lifetime. And I say to you that that may be why you have so much anger and hate toward the opposite race.

What if all Jewish people realized that they were all Germans in the last lifetime, and all the German people realized that they were all Jewish people in the last lifetime? What if all the Indians realized that they were all white in their last lifetime and the whites realized that they were all Indians in their last lifetimes as well? Wouldn't that be an interesting concept for you to struggle with about your own DNA and your own heritage? I say to you, the truth will set you free. Open your eyes, open your mind, because knowledge is the only thing that keeps the mind alive, knowledge and wisdom. The more you desire to learn, the greater your mind and the longer your life will be. As Ramtha insists: "You know, life is the gift of nature, but a lovingly beautiful life is the gift of wisdom."

CHAPTER FIVE
A True Story about Prejudice

common thought is reality

"If you are a revengeful person, you have hate in your heart, that is a seed and it flowers common thought from it. Then an everyday exchange has an opportunity to be a flowering of a life. Here we have a flowering of poison, literally. That is the garden; that is the consciousness that is flowering — I mean, in some of you. Well, that common thought is reality. And the ideal is that if we can open up your chest, tear out all of the garbage that is in it, burnish those shelves and put one beautiful, brilliant thing there that that becomes the ulterior motive, then the flowering of common thought from that will be assured that you will have a magical life and a sweet life, a life that is empowered, that is one with nature instead of warring against it, a life that allows the dream to come about quickly."

— Ramtha

I want you to consider a few thoughts from my interview with Glen, the father of Tiffany, whom we interviewed earlier. This is his story in his own words.

Glen admits that he hates white people. I get the feeling he is not too fond of blacks either. He never did get around to stating exactly why he hates whites, though his story reveals several interesting possible reasons.

My point is that he has never answered that question for himself, never dealt with his feelings or his attitudes. I told Glen I thought he held onto his hate because it was easier than changing. He agreed.

This is his life; this is how he wants to live it. So the question that remains for us is what do we want for our life? Consider this interesting true story:

Glen: Cheryl and I have broken up and made up more times than most couples have even talked on the phone. She knows me, everything about me. She has seen me angry. She has seen me sick and beat up. She has seen me crying and she has seen me drunk. She knows my potbelly and she knew me when I was slim and trim. I have been in jail, on drugs, and she has seen all of that. What else is there for her to go through but for us to love each other?

I don't like white people; I can't stand them. But I love her. And if I had to do it again, I would never marry another white girl. And if you back up to 1969 when we got married, I won't marry a white girl. But I would marry Cheryl.

Sir Robert: So you don't see Cheryl as really a color.

Glen: No, I see Cheryl as my wife, as my woman, friend, buddy, partner. Thirty-one years of marriage puts us in a special fraternity.

Sir Robert: Why don't you like white people?

Glen: I don't like white people. They are back-stabbing snakes. I don't like any of them. And I am fifty-three and I don't like them.

Sir Robert: How do you see them, as white devils?

Glen: White devils? That is an understatement. Look at your politicians. Look at what is going on in the world. Look at how whitey conquers and divides. I don't trust them. I trust Cheryl because I know her. This is prejudice. I am prejudiced. When I see a white boy on the street, I don't trust him. And I grew up with white boys.

When I was four or five years old, I lived in a neighborhood with a bunch of white boys, and we would play together. All of a sudden this little German family moved in, a boy and a girl. They had a fence around their house and they had all the latest toys and the greatest toys. Every one of my white friends could go in their yard and play with their toys, except for me. They wouldn't let me in. I didn't understand, so I used to hang on the fence and watch them play.

My grandson is six. About three months ago he was playing with some little boys. And an older white boy walked up to him and insisted he do something really despicable if he wanted to play with his little friends.

Sir Robert: Where was this?

Glen: This was in Yelm, Washington, an eleven-year-old white boy. Well, guess what? My grandson did what he asked because all he wanted to do was to play with them. Now are you going to tell me about white people? Now you know why I don't like them.

I learned one thing a long time ago: They have got the money. If you want to get the money, you have got to deal with them. But I don't like them. They are some downright coyote-snake-dogs that don't like niggers. And that is prejudice. They don't even know you. They just don't like you because their parents told them that you are nasty. The only reason white girls like brothers is because the parents said he has got a dick that is this big. That is the truth. That is why the white girls during slavery went and got the brothers out of the slave compound, because the master told the white girl that the brothers got big dicks.

My mother and father, my grandfather, my grandmother never, ever advocated any prejudice or racism. I can't remember any outward expression in the early years that formed my personality, my character. I learned it through experiences.

Sir Robert: Do you see that the Jamaican and the Africans all see themselves as a better class than black Americans?

Glen: Yes, because they weren't born in America. Today the Chinese, Vietnamese, Colombians all think they are better than us and they think we are spoiled, rotten brats, and we are. But my dad was upper-middle-class black Jamaican, and my mom was lower-middle-class black American.

All of my cousins were very light-skinned. I was the darkest one. And my grandmother and grandfather showed animosity toward me because I was dark-skinned. My grandmother looked like a white girl. You see, here is the racism setting in. My grandmother was from Indiana, as white as Cheryl. My grandfather was dark, dark, from Arkansas.

Sir Robert: It doesn't fit, because you love your wife and you didn't have the indoctrination of prejudice. As a teenager being liked by whites, being the star amongst whites, what made you become so bitter?

Glen: I was the better star on the football field, but there were black athletes whose fathers had more influence with the mayor and stuff. They were upper-middle-class. That is what happened. White folks influence politics; money talks. This is when I started to realize I had some white boys in my corner, because I was the fastest and won the contests. This is what saved me from the real hard-core brother that was in the streets — sports.

When I was eight or nine, I was held down by a couple of

white boys in YMCA Camp and was raped by another white boy. But I was vengeful; I messed him up. And this is when I started getting in trouble, but I never told anybody what had happened. Nobody would believe a little black brother.

I really didn't start hating white people until I moved to Washington State where we are today. I got into real estate. I have had to work harder all my life to prove myself to have more talent and more personality as a real estate agent in Washington State. Now we are going back to the question, do you know the difference between covert and overt racism and prejudice? It goes back to 1967 when I dropped out of college and the Black Power movement was going strong. I was hanging out with all of the militant brothers from the north side of Minneapolis. I joined the Black Power; it was called The Way. And Cheryl is still my woman.

The Way taught me how to rap in front of white people about oppression, because the first thing white people ask me is what is it like to be black. This is my woman. She is in my corner all the way. We went through all kinds of stuff. This is my woman, and I am a black militant now.

Sir Robert: So what did they say about you having a white woman?

Glen: They didn't know.

Sir Robert: Why didn't you tell them?

Glen: Because I am not going to burn that bridge, because this woman has been through rough years with me — being with other women, being in jail, getting into fights. I was not into drugs yet at this point. So I got a little militant, in a little trouble. I went to the workhouse in Minneapolis, not into jail really. You go out and go to work, and at night you come back and sleep there.

Now my little brother is coming up, and he is taking after his big brother. The Way is a Black Power movement on the south side. Guess what: It is run by a white man. They were using the blacks. They were pulling in forty, fifty thousand dollars of government money, giving blacks peanuts to go out and do stupid things that would land them in jail.

But they were coming from their soul about wanting to change the world. We were drinking the whiskey and smoking the dope and snorting the coke, and the white man was giving them money; but they were handling the brothers on the north side. So they decide they are going to put together a south-side organization, and a white boy, ex-Catholic priest, handles it and becomes in charge of forty-five militant brothers. This is before Martin Luther King, Jr. and Malcolm X got killed.

In the workhouse, this white boy would pick me up in the morning and turn me loose during the day. I would hit the streets; I would have fun; I would hook up with Cheryl. And at night he would pick me up and take me back to the workhouse, every day for ninety days. He would pick me up on Saturday, drive me over to The Way, and Cheryl would come over. And then at night he would take me back to the workhouse. Sunday I had to stay all day. But six days a week for three months, a white boy was in my corner.

Sir Robert: He was getting paid to do this?

Glen: No, he liked me as a person because I had potential. I worked after high school and I dropped out of college. The kicker is north side, all the militant black brothers, the leader was dating a white girl and he had a black wife. He preached that they were devils. He would go on stage in these churches. We organized a black food program. We would get collections from all the people who felt guilty in white churches and distribute all the food out to the black people. But after a while, the brothers in the program were getting all the donations. This is my Black Power experience. They were taking the money home, two, three hundred dollars a day, with the other six hundred going to the churches.

When they found out I was dating a white girl, they wanted me to get rid of her. I said she had been in my corner for years, but they were only concerned that she was white. So this white- boy priest would sneak me around because the brothers were getting ready to mess me up. So I told them I broke up with her, but this white boy knew we were together and he helped me hook up with her. He gave me money and gave me food to take home to my mother.

Sir Robert: Why don't you like white people? How does the way they are affect you?

Glen: I learned back when I was seventeen that if I want to make any money, I have got to deal with white people, duplicate their success. I am more militant and more angry at fifty-two. You know, I love white people and I hate them. There is a thin line between love and hate. I love my wife. Most of the stuff you see on television is about child abuse from whites. I went to school in North Dakota with them.

And you want to know when I started hating them. I went to work for Town and Country Real Estate Agents in 1996. And I am the only black agent in that office of seventy-five agents.

You have been around a bunch of white people for a long time. You don't have a clue what is going on. You grew up like I did. You know what is up. But I am going to tell you straight up — but I don't like Ram and I don't like your white folks — I don't like nobody but me. I have got three or four people in my life and that is it.

You think you are Gods. You're not. Why don't you just believe in what you have got going on with yourself? You're down here just like I am. I respect you because you are black and that is it. You have got a white girl just like I do. I don't like white people and I don't like the Ram. Why should I have to pay $1,350 dollars a year to get righteous? Why are you paying money if the truth is free? And you've got ninety percent white people there don't even know Ram is black. I have not been impressed by some of the people who come out from the Ram. When I am impressed, I will go to the Ram.

Sir Robert: You should not make your assumptions on people that you meet because after all we are evolving entities as well. You can never judge the message from observing the students. You should be wise and want to make your judgments from your own firsthand experience.

You never know; you may go and learn something that I didn't, and then you can teach me what you learned that I didn't learn, which I am always open for great knowledge. And about believing in what I have going on, until I met Ramtha it was the same mundane thing that every human believed in, and that's keeping up with the Joneses. How boring. What about learning about quantum physics and how the Observer affects subatomic particles and reality? What about learning why you came back to this earth? What about learning about your unfinished business? What about mastering all of your limitations? What about being able to love all creeds and colors? What about being able to love all living things, including yourself?

This to me seems like it would be a greater cause and a greater time spent in life than holding on to secondhand judgments and prejudice. After all, I used to think like you think; what a change!

Glen: I don't like white people because they stab you in the back. They get in your business and they pretend to like you. If you get out there and get a hundred white folks, there are maybe four or five that like you and that is it. I am burned out on the other ninety-five and I am sick of them. They are two-faced.

I had eighty thousand dollars in deals. I am a real estate agent; I can make it work for you. I have got two brokers in my corner. One is on the board of control over the listings. I had a white boy beat me out of the forty-four-hundred-dollar deal and I went to them and they said they would check it out. But he went to the board too. I worked for six months to close another deal and the woman wouldn't pay my commission. I went to my broker. She said I would have to take it to civil court. If I had been white, my broker would have been all over it, but because I am a brother, he didn't do anything. That is my livelihood. I went through that six or seven times. I am out here in the country with all of these white people and I am tired of it. I don't like white people because there are different rules made for us.

The only reason I am in Washington State, the only reason I am up here talking to you is because I love my wife and I have a daughter and a grandson; otherwise I would be in Los Angeles someplace. I could be downtown buying my grandson a piece of candy and some skinhead comes by and blows me away or blows him away. I can go to the sheriff and they will tell me they will go after this guy and they will get him, but what they are really saying is, "It is just another nigger."

White folks stink. They want to be like me, act like me, walk like me, dress like me, part their hair like me, fuck like me, lay in the sun and get a tan. But they are not like us. But we have to act like them because they have all the money. But they are wrong in the head.

This following is an interesting interview with a Jewish woman. Check it out:

Sir Robert: Do you think because you are a Jewish person that you are more special than any other race?

Ruth: I was raised to think that way but not openly admit it.

Sir Robert: Does it really make a difference if it is openly or not openly admitted? After all, isn't it all about our thoughts that create our life?

Ruth: The difference is the hypocrisy and the lies.

Sir Robert: To yourself, or to others as well — the front that you put up?

Ruth: Both. It is masked in a veneer of liberalism and charitable activity.

Sir Robert: Out of all the cultures, which culture are you magnetized to the most?

Ruth: I am magnetized more to blacks because they are freer and not phony.

Sir Robert: When you think of a black person, what is your first thought?

Ruth: They are stupid, poor, and victims.

Sir Robert: Why do you feel obligated, and your family, to assist black people; is it out of guilt?

Ruth: Guilt, yes, and there is also a feeling of kinship in being a victim.

Sir Robert: Since you have been in Ramtha's School of Ancient Wisdom, what have you learned, and how do you feel now?

Ruth: I have learned about the greed and tyranny of the Hebrews in Israel, the injustice of taking Palestine, "killing every living thing that breathed," as stated in the Old Testament as Jehovah's command. I was raised to think it was the Hebrews' right and that it was a glorious event when the Hebrews conquered Palestine. I have since learned that the Palestinians were a peaceful people and had created a land of milk and honey; as Ramtha mentioned, they had grapes the size of cantaloupes.

The Hebrews took forty years to go less than three hundred miles in their Exodus from Egypt. When Ramtha has said — and I have confirmed it by looking at the maps myself — that it is only a two-and-a-half hour drive in an SUV, clearly forty years was enough time for Jehovah to create a group of blind, crazy people who appear to have submitted themselves and done whatever he said. And what bothers me most is the hypocrisy today of Jewish people who say today they believe in civil rights and yet they still believe the Jews are the chosen people with a special right to live in Israel, which was Palestine, as well as regard themselves as a moral superiority — as if Jews are morally or intellectually superior to other races.

What gives them that right? Palestine was already the home of a peace-loving people. That is why the suicide bombers are willing to die. Wouldn't you fight back if someone came to your home with a gun and told you they were taking over? I have also learned to see my own greed and obsession with money, which I had never seen before. And I had always thought I was so charitable, and yet if you give with an expectation of return, a condition, a judgment on the recipient as being less-than, or a hope to relieve your own guilt, that is not charitable giving. It is not unconditional love.

The Jews, I believe, have made a religion out of money and the power it has given them. Abraham had great wisdom and knew how to manifest great things, but his powers were subverted into a love of the material manifestations and a loss of the ultimate goal of gaining wisdom. I have also learned of the weight of judgment, of thinking of yourself as superior, and the harm it causes to yourself, because your soul does not desire that. It desires wholeness and harmony.

Sir Robert: I ask you what you have learned now since you have had an opportunity in your life to spend time with blacks?

Ruth: To think of oneself as superior is to cut oneself off from potential experience and joy. To live with judgment or a self-righteousness about being a victim is to manifest all of that in your own life, for what you observe, you create. It is best not to identify with any religious or ethnic identities, for we are just born into this life, body and culture, to learn what we didn't learn before.

Sometimes I am afraid of the choice of this culture in this lifetime, for there is still much in it to be addressed and owned. I ask myself, how in my life would I be taking a forty-year journey to go less than three hundred miles distance? Luckily, I have been exposed to Ramtha's School of Ancient Wisdom where the constraints and limitations that often prevent us from growing and evolving as human beings, which we have inherited from our cultures, are openly addressed. Through conscious reflection and observation I have gained the tools to change as a human being and move beyond cultural borders that divide and separate us. I am grateful for my soul's persistence in this matter of personal evolution.

Sir Robert: Now back to the question. What have you learned?

Ruth: I have learned a joy in being, a joy in being in the moment as opposed to being intellectual. I have learned a joy in experience, even as simple as eating good food and enjoying good music and laughter. I have learned not to judge people's experience and the color of their skin and to allow people their own journey. I have a sense that black people are really alive; they are not afraid of speaking their truth. From my experience, if you were black and educated, then you were acceptable, even impressive. Academic achievement and approval of the community in that sense has been so important in the Jewish culture. I don't regret having emphasized my schooling but now know it was a waste to judge others who didn't have it, as if somehow they were not wise enough.

Sir Robert: Do you think God chooses if one is worthy for the kingdom of heaven by their intellect? Do you think God sees all humankind as equal?

Ruth: God sees all humankind as equal. Being merely an intellectual I see now as more of a hindrance to becoming a powerful creative God.

Sir Robert: But it is also a tool to be politically correct in a way.

Ruth: Yes, you can find the right words to impress someone in a particular moment, but you are left feeling empty or maybe self-righteous because you succeeded.

Sir Robert: Don't you think that God, the Source of all life, is looking for something greater? And that would be the fulfillment of the soul's desire and the conquest of unfinished business that prevent us from continuing our journey of evolution. From this point of view, the reason why all creeds and colors are battling back on the face of the earth is so they can provide the playground, the stage, as Shakespeare said, where everyone can have the opportunity to play the role they need to play, learn from it, and move on. Would you agree with this interpretation or disagree?

Ruth: I agree.

Sir Robert: Then I say to you, welcome to chaos and change, to striving for the kingdom of heaven.

Ruth: Bring it on. So be it.

CHAPTER SIX
*Stop Being Black
and Be an Individual*

when we love ourselves enough

"But, you see, joy is a release and it is also a wisdom, and that is what we get when we love ourselves enough to tackle our difficulties. To expect someone else to do it for us is meaningless. I, as your Teacher, will not make you happy. I am here to tell you what you are — and you get to make choices from that — and to give you excellent knowledge that you can start to integrate, and to give you hope, and to keep reminding you I am talking to Gods out here. I am talking to immortals that are so powerful that they can believe themselves into eternal death. That is how powerful you are. I am talking to Gods."

— Ramtha

Our children are so special. We should all love all races, colors, and creeds of children. They are so wise. We as adults think we know so much more, but we are so wrong. They are so pure and innocent, and they are so determined to be free. Let them be free. Listen to them. Listen to their desires and their requests. I have learned to do so. Don't judge them because you don't understand them or because you no longer laugh with the freedom of a child. Try to find their level. Never take their joy from them.

Let us teach your children that for every choice there is another choice. Let us teach them to be conscious of their choices. I was so demanding of my oldest two children. I didn't listen to them and allow them their own choices. You can learn from the smallest child you have in your family. Don't be too busy, too caught up in making money that you miss the wisdom that comes from listening to our children. They fully believe that God is. They will teach you to be happy and to love. They will teach you to play. Don't think you are too important to have a childlike attitude.

Everyone has chosen their experience in this lifetime. Let us give our children room to have their experience. So many times I wanted to stop my children when I saw the road they were going down. But if I did, what lessons would they learn? Would they learn to be responsible for their own creations or would they have to come back and experience it all over again? When I contemplated that, I let them go the way they chose. I can only tell them what I see in their choices, what I think might happen. I respect their choices because who am I to stop them? I have not been happy with all of their choices. Sometimes my first reaction has been "no."

Instead, I say, "Bear with me. Let me contemplate what you bring to me. Let me take it to my God, and I will talk with you tomorrow." And if I don't catch myself, my children catch me. They know they have the free will and the power to do what they choose to do.

My only choice, in order to feel comfortable in my soul, is to say "So be it. You should experience your desire. Go with a light heart. Be wise and take everything that you have been taught from your great Teacher, Ramtha, and apply it in your life." Our children today will be the parents of tomorrow, and we must take time to understand them and allow them to express themselves however they feel is necessary.

The black man should take responsibility for his children and not be a victim and leave it up to the black woman to take care of their children. I was raised by nothing but women. You can find this to be true of over seventy-five or eighty percent of all black children. The men desert the women for one reason or another, for one excuse or another, and leave it up to the black women to raise the children.

I never resented being raised by my mother, my grandmother, my sisters, and my brothers — mainly my auntie, my mother, and my grandmother. They were the strong force in my lifetime, raising me as a child, and I loved them greatly. Sure, my mother had men in her life to come into her life and assist her. I did not meet my father until I was thirty-four years of age. And I say to you, black men, look around. Why are we as black men becoming victims and becoming less than the men that we are, to take responsibility for the seed that we laid that brought forth the children?

Brothers, it is time to wake up and to own your children, to take responsibility for your children and to be a part of their lives every step of the way. You owe that to them and you owe that to yourself. You brought them into this world and it was no accident. There is no such thing as an accident. The genetics of the mother of your child and of you, the father of your child, were not an accident. It was chosen intentionally by the child to be raised by you both.

So I say to you, stop using excuses. Stop having everyone else take care of your children and then complain about them, and bitch and complain about what you don't have, and complain about what you can or cannot do, and about why you? I say to you, black brothers, that you were man enough — or boy enough — to put that penis in that vagina and create that baby. So it is up to you to take care of what you created, of what both of you created. And that is why I have always had a greater respect for the women in the world than I do for the men, because the women are the backbone of all of our lives. Without them, we would not live today.

Men, let's not say that women are stronger behind closed doors and in public say that they are weaker than you. The truth of the matter is that you are the weak one, to give them the seed, the sperm, and then leave it up to them to raise the baby. Men, we as black men, we as men of the world have to be greater and stronger and have a greater mind than our first seal, our penis that runs rampant, that has no brain and cannot think. We have to be greater than that and go back. If each man would go back and take responsibility for the children that they have brought into this world, a lot of the women would be off of welfare — a lot of them would be off the welfare. So it is about the men going back and taking responsibility for their children, doing whatever you can do for them. But don't — don't — leave it on the shoulders of just the women and expect them to do it.

And I say to you, brothers — and when I say brothers, I am talking about all men in the universe — I say to you, brothers, that we must take back the responsibility for our young, for our offspring, the ones that will be the light to the world in our future. They desire to be a part of our life or they would never have chosen us. They would never have chosen the woman and the man that put together the sperm and the egg that offered them the opportunity of a new life. It would never have happened if it were not for the strength of that soul desiring the right mix from both to be in his life.

If you were abandoned by your father, it is no excuse for you to abandon your children today. You could have been abandoned by your father or your mother, but you are strong, you are healthy, you are successful — whatever that means to you — or you are satisfied in life. So it is no excuse for you to do the same to your offspring. We are supposed to be greater and wiser than what was done to us, that we don't perpetuate it on our offspring. So we should go back, humble ourselves, and take responsibility for what we have brought into this world — without guilt. No guilt, my brothers. Don't go back with any guilt; go back with the desire to take back your responsibility that you have started in this lifetime. And if they are grown up and you have not been in their lives, ask permission to come into their lives and do whatever you can do for them as grown individuals.

We have to earn the right to be a father. It is easy to make a baby, but we have to earn the right for a child to call us father or for a child to call us mother. It is not just automatically done because the spermatozoa and the egg became one and created the baby. No, both. And mainly you men are whom I am talking to; mainly you have to earn the right for any child to desire to call you father.

I have never, ever in my life called any man my father until I met Ramtha the Enlightened One. Only when I met him and felt his love and passion for me did I call him my father, and I mean that from the depths of my heart. But no human man have I ever called father in my life.

Do I have some prejudice against that? Yes, I did, because I always wanted a father. I always wanted a father to look up to, to help me. But when I met my real father, Ramtha, I realized the purpose of my journey in this lifetime. And I humbly apologize to my father, who is no longer on this plane, that my journey in this lifetime was to come and be born through his DNA and my mother's DNA and to be raised by women, not by men. So this day, in the twenty-first century, I no longer have prejudice against my father. I have no resentment against my late father. I have no resentment against my mother. I love them greatly because I am taking full responsibility for the path that I am walking in my life, that all that I have created in my life and all that has unfolded in my life has been from my own creation for my learning.

So I can't blame my father anymore for not being there because I knew he wasn't going to be there when I chose him from the Plane of Bliss. I can't blame my mother for doing more or doing less because I knew before I chose her that I would be a radical not listening to anyone.

So I say to you that it is all about taking back my power, your power, as a black man, as an individual, to take responsibility for all of our creations in this lifetime that we have partaken in — all of our creations. It is never too late.

Your children may be grown up, but when you go back to them, you be humble and be wise and be willing to just listen to their anger and their bitterness that they have toward you because they wanted you there when you were not there. Understand them for their desire and say nothing, but be humble.

And when it is all over, say to them, "I have been in error, but it was no mistake. I am in error. So I say to you: Can I start from this day forward being the father that brought you into this world, to the best of my ability? And I may stumble and I may fall, but I will get up, if you allow me to take on the responsibility that I have turned my back on. And I cannot make up for the days and the times that I was not there, but I can go from this moment forward and be the best that I can be."

I say, brothers, do this thing; it is worth everything. I don't care who your children are; do this thing. And when you do this, it is one step closer to freeing yourself from your guilty conscience, wondering where they are, wondering who they are, wondering how they are doing, wondering if they are alive or if they are dead. It doesn't matter; be willing to take the responsibility of who and what you have created in this lifetime.

I truly have been an entity in this lifetime that every woman that I have met has asked me or expected me to take care of her children — and I am still not sure what that is all about. But I have always done the best I could do with any child that is a part of my life. I have always loved being with children because to me, in my eyes, children are what God is, with a light heart, no judgment, pure, and laughter. And I have always loved and honored the responsibility of taking care of children with any woman that came into my life, and there have been many.

And I can say to you that my children, my blood children, I have always desired to have full responsibility for them. When I was younger, I was ignorant with my oldest daughter. I was ignorant; I was a victim; I was a tyrant. And she was so much like me that I could not handle her. And because I tried to manipulate her and handle her and control her and she would not hear of it, she left at the age of fifteen on her own.

But to this day I do not feel guilty for what happened. I do not feel guilty. I have no shame for what happened. And I love her greatly to this day. I will do all that I can do for her because when I had her, I was young and I was ignorant. But I am older and wiser today and love her greatly. And I would do anything for her. I will help her see the way to knowing God, and I will help her know that God is her greatest friend and lover — not any man but God in us, as I have learned — the same with all of my children. I love them greatly. And my two next-to-the-youngest children, I have taken full responsibility for them and raised them myself. I have taken full custody of them. They live with me and I have raised them myself, with their mother visiting and intervening and supporting any way she can. I have honored that. But I have made the switch. Rather than their being a burden on her by being with her, they are with me. And I have had a great opportunity to teach them all that I have learned, to teach them about God, to teach them that their greatest lover and friend is the almighty God that exists within them, and to help them learn how to tap into that force within them.

And I have had a great opportunity to introduce them to my father, Ramtha, and they have been with him. My son has been with him since the age of five. The other, my daughter, has been with him since the age of seven. They have maintained themselves current in a school that teaches them they have the power and the freedom to change their life and become a sparkling jewel that contributes to the evolution of humanity, and they love Ramtha greatly, and my youngest son has been with him since he was conceived. Ramtha has taught them greatly to love themselves. He has taught them to be responsible for who and what they are. He has taught them not to be victims, not to be tyrants, not to be emotional wrecks, but to be the Gods that they are, that they are evolving each and every day to be.

I love greatly that I have had the opportunity to share this with Cozette and with Robert, and one day I desire to share it with Maisha and Kristynna as well. And also I have had a great desire and opportunity to share it with my youngest son, Exa-Siltana, the beloved one that knows all.

So I say to you, brothers, I say to you, sisters, if you can't get along with one another that is all right, but put down your judgments and prejudice and think about the love. Think about the survival and the knowledge and the superiority of the child who is greater than you and your spouse. I see my offspring all as being wiser and greater than what I chose to be in this lifetime, and I don't have a problem with that. I will listen to any one of them for advice because they are pure. They have less judgments and prejudice to deal with when we as adults are always thinking whether we are going to win, lose, fail, or be successful. A child merely says how they feel in their mind in the moment. It is so pure and clean and innocent; they are not coming from an altered ego. They are coming from purity.

And, brothers, I say to you, a lot of what we can do for an individual has nothing to do with material things. It has everything to do with just doing and being truthful and honest in the moment with them — just in the moment with them. Your presence, in many cases, will become so much more valuable than any material things you may think you have to give them.

So I say to you, brothers, allow these words to touch your soul. It is beckoning at your soul. Let us not be a fool, be ignorant, but wise, because the very one that you may turn your back on may be the very one that, if you slip up and die in this lifetime, you may come back to and ask to allow you another chance of life, to be their child. Let us not be a fool, my brothers and sisters, and love them.

Don't blame the drugs, my brother, for your not being able to take care of your responsibility, because no drugs have ever killed anyone. The individuals using the drugs have killed themselves. No drug can jump up and get into your system without your helping the drug. Be responsible. Let us take care of our children, love them, honor them, help them, and be there for them. All it takes, my brothers and sisters, is a moment — a moment — to make a choice of change. And call forth God within you to help you and it will be done as quickly as you have made the choice.

You don't have to believe me. Just do it and see what will happen. God will never give you anything on your journey that you cannot handle. I say this to you from the love of my heart, to love all children, to allow all children to have the right and the freedom to be innocent and to be who they are. Let us protect all children and love them, and teach them not prejudice, teach them not a difference from one color to another, but teach them equality and the value of everyone's freedom; that all of us have a common denominator equally within us, and that is the creative power of God and the freedom to exercise it. Let no one teach them differently and make them stand up to the line not wanting anything less than to call forth the God within them to allow them to do all that they deserve to do. I say this to you from the depths of my heart.

You may disagree with what you have heard me say here, about God or the possibility of reincarnation and the consequences it has in the way we see our life, our judgments, and our prejudice. But disagree you may; this is my truth, this is my experience, this is my observation, and this is my life that brought me to who I am today. I have learned that truth — truth — will set you free and will make you hollow and make room for God in your life. When you can speak the truth honestly, no matter what anyone thinks or cares about you, God will open the doors for you and you will have no regret, no sorrow, and no shame. Every moment, every day is a new day, beginning a new day in your life, and you can change.

And, brothers, when I say to you to take back your power, I am not talking about a revolution against whites and other cultures. I am not talking about killing and destroying other life. I am not talking about being a victim or being a tyrant because you chose to be black, male, or female in this lifetime. I am not talking about destroying others because you chose to be poor or rich in this lifetime.

Taking responsibility for life means you have to stop blaming everybody else for your situation. And I don't care what your situation is. Every situation you have in your life is something that you created for a learning experience and at any moment we realize this, it can be changed. And it is time for the whole world and all of the cultures in the world to take responsibility for their own choices, their own lives. You did it; you made the decision.

Number two, who is going to change it? Stop looking outside of yourself. If you don't like it, you must become responsible to change it yourself. Stand up and say I don't like this. This is what I have to do to change it: I am getting off welfare and I am getting a job. I am no longer going to work this job that pays me minimum wage. I am going to educate myself and go out and get a better paying job. I am no longer going to be a victim because I am a woman. I am going to be educated and stand the line to deal with anybody I have to deal with to get where I want to be in life. I am no longer going to use the excuse that my great-great-grandfather was a slave so I am less than anybody else. I am responsible for who I am and what I am doing today. I am no longer going to be a victim because I have all these children and I don't have a husband. I am the only one that can make this situation any better. Even if I only see two possible choices, there are at least ninety-nine others. I no longer blame the woman for the children. I made them too and brought them into the world. I will take responsibility and take care of them. I will seek out what my choices may be.

Most people don't want to be responsible for their lives, for their situation. They want to blame somebody else instead of looking at themselves in every situation that they are in and asking, "Why did I create this?" But looking and asking is the only way to live, about everything. Anything that happens, any situation, I ask myself, "Why did I create this situation? What am I supposed to learn from it? And how could I have done it differently? What will I do about it now?" Then you have power in your life and can start making headway in your life.

Get out of your box means ending a way of thinking that you have learned and that you are comfortable in. I was in a box of thinking that someone who could read was better than me. That is a self-imprisonment. When we go outside the box and say so what, then we find a way to learn to read and to get a job. And if you go at it enough times, you will find a way; then you are out of that box.

Every time we step outside of our box, we shock ourselves that we did. We don't know how we did it, but we did, and

STOP BEING BLACK AND BE AN INDIVIDUAL

your box gets bigger. Then you find a way to step out again. You broaden your box until it is as big as the whole world. But you can only do that when you know that you are responsible for everything that happens in your life.

You can change it if you want to. How can I say that? I have been there; I know that. I have been in prison; I know that. I have been on drugs; I know that. I have been a poor, poor, black man; I know that. Can you get out of it? Yes. I was a nonreader for twenty-nine years. Now I am a writer of books. There is nothing that we have created in this lifetime that we cannot change if we say, "Enough of this. I don't want it anymore. I will change now."

Stop being a black American and be an individual, a God waking up, fully realized, because as I was told by my great Teacher and verified it in my own experience, if you claim to be a black American, an African American, then you take on all the consequences that come with that. Be an individual desiring to know God and be responsible.

Say no to the drugs. Don't tell me you're not strong enough because all you have to do is be consciously aware of what you are doing to the great temple that God has given you — your body — and you will be strong enough to say no to drugs. Say no to alcohol. Say no to the pills. Make up your mind, brothers, that you are greater.

You could say, "How did these drugs get into America? No black man had the power or the money to bring them in," but I also can say then to you that because they bring them in, that doesn't mean that you have to partake of them. There are many of us that don't.

So it is all about making a choice, brothers and sisters. All drugs that you partake of — all drugs that you know are putting an alternate change on your mind and your body, because you feel it — all you have to do is to say no; I am going to be greater than this. All you have to do is step up to the line and call forth the God within you to tell your body: No more. I no longer desire this. I no longer want this in my body. I no longer want this in my life.

And I say to you anything that you ask God to change within you — because your God is not prejudiced — it is a done deal. It is changed. And the more you ask and the quicker you demand, the quicker it is done.

You can change anything, any drug, any alcohol, any pills, overeating, undereating, lousy attitudes, anything at any moment in time, because you created this situation. All you have to do is say, "Lord God of my being, I no longer desire this situation," and it will be changed right away because you are also saying, "I know I created this situation, so I will stop it and change it." But you first have to acknowledge and admit what you have created and become aware.

We as black men who feel that white men can get better jobs than us, it is only because we create such a consciousness and have been creating that consciousness for hundreds of years, that because of the color of our skin, we cannot get what the white man gets or do what the white man does. What if you make up your mind that it is what you want and let nothing stop you, and you let God know what you want, and you walk the path and you make it happen? I say to you that is the real truth and the power within us, not blaming someone else for our lack. Our lack is merely what we have perpetrated upon ourself by being victims.

If you think you are going to be mistreated because of your color, that is the only thing that can happen to you. The other thing is separation: When you listen to anybody that wants to separate the races, then you are talking about one being better than or one being less than. That is a trick too. And I would say that any leader of those cultures, if you want to call them that, that wants to separate you from anybody else, that is something I would question. Why would they want to do that? Because a government will support that? The truth is, that holds us back.

Even when you take a child that is told they have a learning disability, the truth is that the school system is set up to make all kids fail, except for the select few. There are different ways of learning, and very few people learn well by the methods used in public schools. Society is actually set up knowing that if we raise all our kids being able to achieve, then when they graduate, what will they do for jobs? These things are manipulated because somebody has to be the laborers.

In every pack, you will find a rat. But when you have the consciousness, the attitude that you are equal to everyone else, you don't attract in your life people that think you are less than. When that happens, I just send them love. Love is the great equalizer. I just don't buy into it.

It is quite another thing to get the black people of America to see this. The rap music was created to control minds and to keep the people of color down, because the hidden messages in rap music are all about death, sex, and destroying somebody else, and drugs. And every time somebody buys somebody's rap music with this message, they are supporting the cause of the people who are endeavoring to trick them and hold them down.

It is the same thing every time they watch it on television. When you stop and think why would they allow so many people of color to be so successful with such music, It is because they can control the blacks. The blacks are a large minority. Whites are fast becoming the minority in America.

You have such a game being played in this society where you can take some of the who's who in the ghetto, and the government or the man can say, "I will give you X amount of dollars because I believe in you, and I am saying that other minority group over here is trying to belittle you. And I think you should be equal to them. So I will supply the weapons, I will supply the drugs, and I will make it happen so that you organize your people and destroy one another." And guess who you are destroying? Other people like yourself, of color.

There are not too many black men in the world that have been denied to be with a white woman that desire to be with one. And the more famous you get and the more powerful you become, the easier you have access to a white woman that has a desire to be with a black man. So my question has always been, with Martin Luther King, Jr., who taught love and peace and was surrounded with white women, the press put out there that this was a man who had never been with a white woman before in his life. They say the same about Jesse Jackson. But it is an irrelevant point. It is part of a game that has been passed down since slavery, that one race desires the other sexually. So maybe racism isn't as big a thing in this country as we think it is. But as long as a lot of noise is made about it and everybody thinks it is a big thing, it keeps everybody separate and controllable.

Even my own family, coming from twelve sisters and brothers, has such a thing for white people it is unbelievable. I grew up with understandable reasons for fearing and hating whites. To this day, trying to get them to understand that it has nothing to do with color, that it has to do with what you think manifests in your life — that it doesn't have anything to do with the white man — they don't want to take responsibility for that choice. It is easier. As long as they don't have to be responsible, then they never have to change.

I say to all the people in the world, there is nothing you can't manifest if you can hold a passionate thought, like an Oprah Winfrey, like a Whoopi Goldberg, like a Cher, or like a Bill Cosby. They made up their minds that they were going to achieve something in their lives regardless of their creed or color. And they have done it.

How many of you take time every night and give thanks to your God that you are alive? How many of you don't? How many of you wake up in the morning and give thanks to God that you have another day to learn, understand, become enlightened — and how many of you don't?

Know this, brothers; know this, sisters, that I can only say these things to you because I have experienced them. I have walked the walk, talked the talk. I have made changes and taken responsibility.

The rich man is afraid that he is going to be poor. The poor man is afraid that one day he will be rich. There is no difference. And along with his fear that one day he will be rich, he is afraid that one day he will be poor again. What is the difference?

The black men want the jobs to make the money, but they are afraid to step up to the line because of the white man, thinking the white man is greater than what they are. Be an individual and not a follower. Do that and go for what you want. Don't accept no. Go all the way. Realize that from this moment in time forward, all that you do and all that you experience is your choice, and it is neither good nor bad, right nor wrong. It just is and it sets the pace for those who come after us.

And from the "just is," if you have learned from it and never repeat it again, you are free. You are free. And every choice we make, brothers and sisters, we must become more conscious. We must be able to see the action and the reaction that is going to follow, and we must become more responsible as individuals.

But I don't mean separate — separation is not the answer — that only because we are black we get to do certain things or go certain places. That is not the answer. Don't you realize that that is what has been put upon us all of our lives? We call that prejudice, yet within our own race and our own culture, our own selves, we promote separation. We have to stop it and promote oneness, one consciousness in God.

All men and all women and all colors should say my brothers and sisters, not just black men and black women. If you do, you create separation, a less than and a greater than, the same thing we have been arguing and complaining about for two hundred years. We are doing it ourselves. Freedom is equality to all kinds, all cultures, all races, as the fathers of the Constitution intended when they set the foundation of our great country. Do not separate yourself.

Do not see yourself as better or as lesser. See yourself as the equal that you are.

And when we can do this, we can make great changes. We can depend upon no one but ourselves and the power of our God in us. One of the greatest things that I love about my Teacher, Ramtha, is when he insists that he is not our savior but that we are our only savior, and that he is not here to be worshiped but to worship the God that we have forgotten is who we really are.

Stop and think, brothers. It makes no difference what color his skin is. If there is an entity so clear on what he is doing and why he is here — and I swear to you, there is — he has stepped up to the line to teach us how he has taken his body back to from whence he came and never died. He has taught us that we have the same power and we should all live an eternal life, never dying. Our body is the greatest vehicle ever created, but who we truly are is our mind.

The great thing that has given us the opportunity for this life is women, our mothers, our wives, our sisters, our aunties — Mother Nature. That is so much more powerful than what we are, men. When you look at your wife again, contemplate her power, her passion, her love, and her concern, and respect her for it. Respect her, because we may have muscles and be strong, but we are not strong enough to bring forth life. We are not strong enough to go nine months and bring forth a baby. And if you ever want to see an experience, men, of power, experience a birth. Watch a birth. Watch your woman bring forth a baby and you will see power. Then you will ask the question, could I have done that? Obviously not. So it is time for us to respect the women, and love the women, and see women as our equal, as human beings with a mind, a soul, and a Spirit.

And I say to you once again, I can only speak this because I have spoken it to myself first. I will continue to do that and to learn. All that I say to you, I can say because I said it to myself first. Don't think that because I write a book that I am better or different than you. The only thing that is different is that I have walked the walk and am now sharing with you what I know. I am consciously aware of it and I have changed it, and I continue to change it daily, every moment, every second. To be responsible is to be free, yet never forget to have joy and a light heart.

I love Ramtha's words when he says, "The greatest of things are achieved in a light heart." I will finish our little reflection on prejudice with this. I have tried it; believe me, it works.

LETTERS OF RECOGNITION

WHOOP, INC.

Burbank, California 91522

August 29, 1988

Robert D. Jones, Jr.
I BEAT DYSLEXIA, INC.
4306 Crenshaw Boulevard, Suite 100
Los Angeles, CA 90008

Dear Robert:

Having grown-up with the condition of Dyslexia, I know what a struggle getting through life can be.

If I BEAT DYSLEXIA, INC. can bring light to one Dyslexic and information to one non-Dyslexic, then your mission will be complete.

I trust the numbers will be much higher and wish you every success with this most worthy project.

Very truly,

Whoopi Goldberg

Linda Evans

May 9, 1993

Mr. Robert D. Jones, Jr.
Dyslexia, Inc.
P.O. Box 50
Rainier, WA 98576

Dear Robert:

Thank you so much for making me aware of the tremendous and overwhelming problem of illiteracy and children and adults suffering with dyslexia.

The work you are doing at Dyslexia, Inc. with your "I Beat Dyslexia" program is outstanding!

I support you and your efforts and am proud to be associated with your organization.

Sincerely,

June 1, 1993

Mr. Robert D. Jones, Jr.
President
Dyslexia, Inc.
P.O. Box 50
Rainier, WA 98576

Dear Robert:

I wanted to share with you the benefits that I have gained from taking the Instructors Course of "I BEAT DYSLEXIA".

Much to my surprise, the techniques used in your class not only gave me a new awareness of why the approaches used in our schools do not apply to people with dyslexia, but taught me that this approach needs to be addressed immediately.

Your course has made me consciously aware of the problems of adults and children with learning disabilities and that there is hope and help.

I offer my continued support in any way you deem useful.

I look forward to teaching and making these changes in my own life.

Cordially,

Ann Davis, Ph.D.
Certified Instructor
Ph.D. Phsyco/Biology
Ph.D. Doctrine of Theology

THE WHITE HOUSE

WASHINGTON

July 30, 1993

Dyslexia, Inc.
Post Office Box 50
Rainier, Washington 98576

Dear Friends:

Thank you for your kind message and enclosure.

I have been deeply moved by the support from people all across the Nation. I appreciate the concern and interest that prompted you to remember me in such a thoughtful fashion.

Sincerely,

Bill Clinton

Selected Bibliography

Epperson, A. Ralph. *The Unseen Hand, An Introduction to the Conspiratorial View of History.* Arizona: Publius Press, 1985.

Frady, Marshall. *Jesse Jackson: A Biography.* New York: Random House, 1996.

Gardell, Mattias. *In the Name of Elijah Muhammad: Louis Farrakhan and the Nation of Islam.* North Carolina: Duke University Press, 1996.

Jensen, Derrick. *The Culture of Make Believe.* New York: Context Books, 2002.

Jones, Jr., Sir Robert D. *I Beat Dyslexia, So Can You.* Yelm: JZK Publishing, a division of JZK, Inc., 2000.

Knight, JZ. *A State of Mind, My Story.* New York: Warner Books, 1987.

Make Gentle the Life of this World. The Vision of Robert F. Kennedy. Edited by Maxwell Taylor Kennedy. New York: Broadway Books, 1998.

Ramtha, A Beginner's Guide to Creating Reality. Revised and Expanded ed. Yelm: JZK Publishing, a division of JZK, Inc., 2000.

Ramtha, The Mystery of Birth and Death: Redefining the Self. Yelm: JZK Publishing, a division of JZK, Inc., 2000.

Ramtha, The White Book. Revised and Expanded ed. Yelm: JZK Publishing, a division of JZK, Inc., 2001.

Rekdal, Paisley. *The Night My Mother Met Bruce Lee.* New York: Vintage Books, a division of Random House, 2000.

Sasson, Jean. *Princess, a True Story of Life behind the Veil in Saudi Arabia.* California: Windsor-Brooke Books, 2001.

Steinem, Gloria. *Revolution from Within: A Book of Self-Esteem.* New York: Little Brown and Company, 1992.

The Autobiography of Malcolm X. Edited by Alex Haley. New York: Ballantine Books, 1964.

The Autobiography of Martin Luther King, Jr. Edited by Clayborne Carson. New York: Warner Books, 1998.

The Speech of Chief Seattle. Speech delivered in 1854 during the treaty negotiations with the governor of Washington Territory. Massachusetts: Applewood Books, 2000.

Index

A

Abraham, patriarch of Israel 116
adult high school 35
Afghanistan 80
Africa 71, 90
African American 61, 72, 89-90, 94, 109, 133, 135
Africans 60, 109
AIDS 96
America 37, 109, 133, 135
American Indian 82
Americans 44, 71
Arabs 54, 62, 72

B

Baptist Church 19, 32, 54
Baptist Sunday School 33
black churches 39, 54
Black Panthers, the 59, 110
blasphemy 32, 90
brain 35, 37, 51, 74, 90

C

C rations 41
C&E^{SM} 50
California 54, 58
Calvary Baptist Church 37
Catholic Church 19, 29, 32, 37, 54, 72, 111
Catholic schools 37
channeling 49-51, 55
Cher (actor) 136
Chicago 42
Chief Seattle 82
Chinese 40, 72, 109
Chinese American 19
Christian Church 32
Clinton, Bill (former president) 36
cocaine 111
Colombians 109
communism 37
confession 32
Congress 36
consciousness 65-66, 134-135, 137
Consciousness & Energy^{SM} 49
Cosby, Bill (actor) 136
culture 17-20, 38, 43, 52-53, 57, 59, 61, 72, 76-77, 80, 89-91, 93, 97, 99-100, 114, 116-117, 123, 131, 134, 137

D

Detroit, Michigan 93-94
devil, the 33
divinity 50, 64, 89-90, 99
DNA 96, 100, 126
drugs 63, 65, 96, 108, 130, 133-135
dyslexia 35-36, 64

E

Egypt 115
Egyptians 64
Einstein, Albert 35
Elliott, Jane (teacher) 20
emergency room 25
equality 38, 40-41, 43-44, 53-54, 56, 58, 61, 63, 71-72, 79, 81, 90, 94, 98, 100, 117, 130, 135, 137
eternal life 33, 138

Europe 77
Exodus, the 115-116

F

Farrakhan, Louis (religious leader) 59
fathers of the Constitution, the 137
Filipino 40
France 56
free will 19, 34, 52-53, 59-61, 64-66, 78, 81, 83, 96, 99, 123-124, 127, 131
freedom 43, 57, 61, 63, 72, 77-81, 96, 99, 123, 130, 137
freedom of religion 81
French 72, 77

G

genetics 73-74, 100
Germans 54, 60, 76, 100, 108
Germany 56
GI Bill for education 35
God 32-33, 35, 37-40, 44, 50-51, 53-54, 56, 58-61, 63, 65-66, 76, 80-83, 89, 97, 117, 123-124, 128, 130-131, 133-134, 138
Goddesses 99
Gods 50, 99, 112, 129
Goldberg, Whoopi (actor) 136
gonorrhea 97
good and evil 38
government 39, 58-59
government aid programs 58-59, 110, 134-135
gynecology 93-94, 97-98

H

Harley Davidson 42
Hawthorne Elementary School 26-27
healing 51
heaven 38

Hebrew 64
hell 33, 38
Henry Ford Hospital, Detroit 94
history 43, 57, 76, 81
homosexuality 65
human rights 40, 81, 115, 130
hysterectomy 95

I

I Beat Dyslexia Center 36
illiteracy 33-35, 40, 132-133
India 80
Indians 54, 59, 62, 100
infantry unit 41
Iowa 20
Iraq 80
Irish 72, 77
Islam 59, 72
Israel 115
Italy 56

J

Jackson, Jesse (civil-rights leader) 136
jail 34, 43, 107, 110-111
Jamaica 72, 77, 109
Japanese 40, 54
Jehovah 115
Jehovah's Witnesses 54
Jesus Christ 31, 39-40, 54, 64
Jews 31, 54, 62, 65, 72, 76, 90, 100, 114-117
JZ Knight 49-52, 55

K

Kansas City 25-26, 42
karma 61
kindergarten 33
King, Jr., Martin Luther 20, 111, 136
kingdom of heaven 82-83, 117-118
knowledge 43, 52, 62-64, 90, 93, 101, 113

INDEX

Korean 40, 54
Kosovo 80
Ku Klux Klan 26

L

Last Supper, the 54
Latin 37
life review 53
long-term memory 36
Louisiana 41

M

mahogany people 89
Malcolm X 111
marijuana 42, 111
medical school 93, 97
Mexicans 54, 80, 100
Middle East 72
military 34-35, 41-42
mind 79, 81, 96, 99-100, 125, 133-134, 138
mind control 96, 115, 135
Mormon Church, the 60
Mother Nature 62, 138

N

Navajo Indians 72
Netherlands 56
neuronet 35, 52, 74
New York City 42
Northern Ireland 80
Norway 56
Norwegian 19, 60-61
nuns 29, 37

O

Observer, the 80, 113, 134
Old Testament, the 115

P

Pakistan 80
Palestine 115
Pentagon, the 96
Philadelphia 42
Plane of Bliss, the 49, 53, 127
police, the 26-27, 39, 114
Pope, the 32, 38
prayer 33, 54, 136
priesthood 32, 37-38, 111
Protestant Church 72

Q

quantum physics 81, 113

R

Ramtha 17-18, 43, 49-53, 55, 65, 76, 101, 112-113, 115, 124, 126, 129, 138-139
Ramtha's School of Enlightenment 49-50, 55, 59, 74, 115-116
rap music 135
rape 30
Red Guard 50, 56
reincarnation 20, 40-41, 44, 49-50, 52-54, 57, 60, 62-65, 80, 90, 100, 116, 123, 126, 131
Rekdal, Paisley (UW Professor) 19
religion 80-82, 89, 98, 116-117, 123
religious ministers 32-33, 38

S

sachems 82
school system, the 39-40, 75, 134
Scottish 72, 77
Seattle, Washington 19
segregation 26, 40
senators 36
Seventh Day Adventist Church 32
sexual abuse 32, 98
Shakespeare, William 118
sin 32-33, 38
slavery 52, 57, 65, 72, 76, 90, 99-100, 136

Social Security 36
soul 42, 44, 55-56, 111, 116-117, 124, 126, 130, 138
soul food 42
South Africa 80
Spain 56
spelling 34, 36, 41
spirituality 55, 63, 74, 82-83, 90, 99, 117, 126
Steinem, Gloria (feminist) 98
subatomic particles 113
syphilis 96-97

T

terrorist attack of 9-11 54, 80
The Way (black power movement) 110-111
tongue-tie 33
Town and Country Real Estate 112

U

University of Washington 19

V

Vatican, the 96
Veterans Administration, The 35
Vietcong 43, 72
Vietnam War 34, 41-43
Vietnamese 43, 72, 109

W

walk point 41-42
Washington 110, 114
welfare 59, 125, 132
Winfrey, Oprah (talk-show host) 136
wisdom 43, 52, 54, 63, 65, 101, 116, 123
women's discrimination 37-38, 62, 93-94, 97-99, 132
World War II 60

X

X chromosome. See genetics

Y

Yelm, Washington 36, 49, 108
YMCA 110

Z

zero-point energy. See quantum physics